CONTENTS

STEAMTOWN NATIONAL HISTORIC SITE AUTHORIZATION AND REFORM

HEARING

BEFORE THE

SUBCOMMITTEE ON NATIONAL PARKS, FORESTS AND PUBLIC LANDS

OF THE

COMMITTEE ON NATURAL RESOURCES HOUSE OF REPRESENTATIVES

ONE HUNDRED THIRD CONGRESS

SECOND SESSION

ON

H.R. 3708

A BILL TO REFORM THE OPERATION, MAINTENANCE, AND DEVELOPMENT OF THE STEAMTOWN NATIONAL HISTORIC SITE, AND FOR OTHER PURPOSES

MAY 12, 1994—WASHINGTON, DC

Serial No. 103–88

Printed for the use of the Committee on Natural Resources

U.S. GOVERNMENT PRINTING OFFICE

86–965 WASHINGTON : 1995

For sale by the U.S. Government Printing Office

Superintendent of Documents, Congressional Sales Office, Washington, DC 20402

ISBN 0-16-046712-8

COMMITTEE ON NATURAL RESOURCES

GEORGE MILLER, California, *Chairman*

PHILIP R. SHARP, Indiana
EDWARD J. MARKEY, Massachusetts
AUSTIN J. MURPHY, Pennsylvania
NICK JOE RAHALL, II, West Virginia
BRUCE F. VENTO, Minnesota
PAT WILLIAMS, Montana
RON DE LUGO, Virgin Islands
SAM GEJDENSON, Connecticut
RICHARD H. LEHMAN, California
BILL RICHARDSON, New Mexico
PETER A. DEFAZIO, Oregon
ENI F.H. FALEOMAVAEGA, American Samoa
TIM JOHNSON, South Dakota
LARRY LAROCCO, Idaho
NEIL ABERCROMBIE, Hawaii
CALVIN M. DOOLEY, California
CARLOS ROMERO-BARCELÓ, Puerto Rico
KARAN ENGLISH, Arizona
KAREN SHEPHERD, Utah
NATHAN DEAL, Georgia
MAURICE D. HINCHEY, New York
ROBERT A. UNDERWOOD, Guam
HOWARD L. BERMAN, California
LANE EVANS, Illinois
PATSY, T. MINK, Hawaii
THOMAS J. BARLOW III, Kentucky
THOMAS M. BARRETT, Wisconsin

DON YOUNG, Alaska
Ranking Republican Member
JAMES V. HANSEN, Utah
BARBARA F. VUCANOVICH, Nevada
ELTON GALLEGLY, California
ROBERT F. SMITH, Oregon
CRAIG THOMAS, Wyoming
JOHN J. DUNCAN, JR., Tennessee
JOEL HEFLEY, Colorado
JOHN T. DOOLITTLE, California
WAYNE ALLARD, Colorado
RICHARD H. BAKER, Louisiana
KEN CALVERT, California
SCOTT MCINNIS, Colorado
RICHARD W. POMBO, California
JAY DICKEY, Arkansas

JOHN LAWRENCE, *Staff Director*
RICHARD MELTZER, *General Counsel*
DANIEL VAL KISH, *Republican Staff Director*

SUBCOMMITTEE ON NATIONAL PARKS, FORESTS AND PUBLIC LANDS

BRUCE F. VENTO, Minnesota, *Chairman*

EDWARD J. MARKEY, Massachusetts
NICK JOE RAHALL, II, West Virginia
PAT WILLIAMS, Montana
PETER A. DEFAZIO, Oregon
TIM JOHNSON, South Dakota
LARRY LAROCCO, Idaho
NEIL ABERCROMBIE, Hawaii
CARLOS ROMERO-BARCELÓ, Puerto Rico
KARAN ENGLISH, Arizona
KAREN SHEPHERD, Utah
MAURICE HINCHEY, New York
ROBERT A. UNDERWOOD, Guam
AUSTIN J. MURPHY, Pennsylvania
BILL RICHARDSON, New Mexico
PATSY T. MINK, Hawaii

JAMES V. HANSEN, Utah, *Ranking Republican Member*
ROBERT F. (BOB) SMITH, Oregon
CRAIG THOMAS, Wyoming
JOHN J. DUNCAN, JR., Tennessee
JOEL HEFLEY, Colorado
JOHN T. DOOLITTLE, California
RICHARD H. BAKER, Louisiana
KEN CALVERT, California
JAY DICKEY, Arkansas

RICHARD HEALY, *Staff Director*
JAMES BRADLEY, *Professional Staff Member*
CHARLENE SEAMENS, *Clerk*
KURT CHRISTENSEN, *Republican Consultant on Public Lands*

STEAMTOWN NATIONAL HISTORIC SITE AUTHORIZATION AND REFORM

THURSDAY, MAY 12, 1994

HOUSE OF REPRESENTATIVES,
COMMITTEE ON NATURAL RESOURCES,
SUBCOMMITTEE ON NATIONAL PARKS, FORESTS
AND PUBLIC LANDS,
Washington, DC.

The subcommittee met, pursuant to call, at 10 a.m., in room 1324, Longworth House Office Building, Hon. Bruce F. Vento (chairman of the subcommittee) presiding.

Mr. VENTO. Let's get started. The Subcommittee on National Parks, Forests and Public Lands will be in order.

Today, the subcommittee is meeting to consider H.R. 3708, the legislation I introduced to both authorize and reform the operation of the Steamtown National Historic Site.

[Text of the bill follows:]

103D CONGRESS
1ST SESSION

H. R. 3708

To reform the operation, maintenance, and development of the Steamtown National Historic Site, and for other purposes.

IN THE HOUSE OF REPRESENTATIVES

NOVEMBER 22, 1993

Mr. VENTO introduced the following bill; which was referred to the Committee on Natural Resources

---

A BILL

To reform the operation, maintenance, and development of the Steamtown National Historic Site, and for other purposes.

Be it enacted by the Senate and House of Representatives of the United States of America in Congress assembled,

TITLE I—STEAMTOWN NATIONAL HISTORIC SITE

SEC. 101. ESTABLISHMENT.

(a) In order to preserve and interpret certain elements of railroading, especially steam-operated railroads during the period of 1850 to 1950, there is hereby established the Steamtown National Historic Site (hereinafter in this title referred to as the "historic site"). The purposes of the historic site shall include interpretation of the evolution of railroads and their impact on the development of this nation, including technological, economic, social, and political effects and the relationship of railroads to industrialization.

(b) The historic site shall consist of the lands and interests in lands within the area generally depicted on the map entitled "Boundary Map, Steamtown National Historic Site", numbered STTO–80,000A, and dated November 1991. The map shall be on file and available for public inspection in the offices of the National Park Service, Department of the Interior. No revisions may be made in the boundary of the historic site, except by Act of Congress.

(c) Sections 1 through 5 of the Steamtown National Historic Site Act of 1986 (Public Law 99–591; 100 Stat. 3341–248–249) are hereby repealed.

SEC. 102. ADMINISTRATION.

The Secretary of the Interior (hereinafter in this title referred to as the "Secretary") shall administer the historic site in accordance with this title and with the provisions of law generally applicable to units of the national park system, including the Act entitled "An Act to establish a National Park Service, and for other purposes", approved August 25, 1916 (39 Stat. 535; 16 U.S.C. 1, 2,

3, and 4). On or before September 30, 1993, the Secretary shall prepare and submit to the Interior and Insular Affairs of the United States House of Representatives and to the Committee on Energy and Natural Resources of the United States Senate a new comprehensive general management plan for the historic site. The plan shall be consistent with this title, with section 12 of the Act of August 18, 1970 (16 U.S.C. 1a–1 through 1a–7) and with other applicable provisions of law.

SEC. 103. ACQUISITION OF LAND.

(a) The Secretary may acquire lands or interests in land within the boundaries of the historic site only by donation or by purchase with donated funds.

(b) The Secretary may not acquire any lands or interests in lands for purposes of the historic site unless such lands are not contaminated with hazardous substances which will require removal or remedial action at the expense of the United States. Any funds of the National Park Service expended, prior to the date of the enactment of this Act, on removal or remedial action with respect to any contamination of lands within the boundaries of historic site shall be fully reimbursed before the Secretary may accept title to any lands for purposes of the historic site. Any such reimbursement shall be credited to miscellaneous receipts in the Treasury. After the full amount of such reimbursement has been credited to miscellaneous receipts, funds expended prior to the date of enactment of this Act by the National Park Service for which such reimbursement was made shall not be treated as amounts expended by the National Park Service for development for purposes of applying the limitation on appropriations for development set forth in section 106.

SEC. 104. PARK SERVICE ACTIVITIES.

(a) The Secretary shall take such actions as necessary and appropriate to administer the historic site, to maintain and preserve the facilities at the historic site, to interpret the resources of the site and their history to the public, and to provide essential services to the public at the historic site.

(b) The Secretary shall preserve the collection of railroad equipment, including locomotives and rolling stock, which is present at the historic site as of the date of enactment of this Act. The Secretary may also preserve such equipment and essential machinery as is necessary for the maintenance of the locomotives and rolling stock. A maximum of 3 steam locomotives and one diesel locomotive may be restored, but only 2 steam locomotives and one diesel locomotive may be operational at any time. The Secretary may not reconstruct or construct new yard equipment or other historic structures or objects. No Federal funds may be expended to provide access between the historic site and any structure that is privately owned and operated for profit. The Secretary may exchange or purchase appropriate examples of locomotives and rolling stock to enhance the site's collection if the total number of such equipment does not increase and if all such actions are consistent with the general management plan for the historic site. The Secretary shall, to the extent practicable, seek donations and assistance from volunteers and other cost-sharing methods to restore the locomotives and rolling stock.

(c) The Secretary shall preserve the artifact collection and archival materials located at the site.

(d) To the extent that it furthers public understanding, and provided that appropriate interpretation is provided, the Secretary may provide a regular excursion from Scranton, Pennsylvania, to Moscow, Pennsylvania. For purposes of such excursions, the Secretary may provide essential visitor services at Moscow, Pennsylvania. The Secretary may not expend funds of the National Park Service for the restoration or maintenance of tracks, bridges or tunnels located outside the historic site, except that the Secretary may use funds appropriated prior to November 15, 1991 for restoration of tracks and bridges between the historic site and Moscow, Pennsylvania, pursuant to a cooperative agreement to be entered into between the Secretary and the owner of such tracks and bridges permitting the national park service to use such tracks and bridges for excursions authorized under this section. The Secretary may pay customary and appropriate track usage fees and may also provide 4 other excursions annually if no such excursion is longer than 50 miles one way.

(e) User fees charged for any rail excursion undertaken shall be established at a level such that a minimum of 75 percent of the costs of maintenance, personnel and equipment for the excursion shall be covered by revenues from the user permit.

(f) The Secretary may assist the owner of Bridge 60 and Bridge 60 Wye with track and switch rehabilitation to facilitate activities associated with the historic site.

(g) The Secretary may enter into cooperative agreements with appropriate authorities for law enforcement and for purposes of controlling rail traffic through the historic site.

SEC. 105. ADVISORY COMMITTEE.

(a) There is hereby established the Steamtown National Historic Site Advisory Committee (hereinafter in this title referred to as the "advisory committee") to provide professional expertise in railroad management and history and advice to the Secretary in the development and operations of the historic site. The advisory committee shall be composed of 11 members appointed by the Secretary to serve for terms of 3 years. The advisory committee shall include 2 experts in the operation of historic railways, 2 experts in the operation of commercial railways, 2 historians of technology, and 2 historians of social history, and 3 members of the general public. Any member of the advisory committee appointed for a definite term may serve after the expiration of his or her term until his successor is appointed. The advisory committee shall designate one of its members as Chairperson.

(b) The Secretary, or his or her designee, shall from time to time, but at least semiannually, meet and consult with the advisory committee on matters relating to the management and development of the site.

(c) The advisory committee shall meet at least 3 times annually.

(d) Members of the advisory committee shall serve without compensation as such, but the Secretary may pay expenses reasonably incurred in carrying out their responsibilities under this title on vouchers signed by the Chairperson.

(e) The provisions of section 14(b) of the Federal Advisory Committee Act (5 U.S.C. Appendix; 86 Stat. 776), are hereby waived with respect to this advisory committee.

(f) The advisory committee shall terminate on the date 10 years after the enactment of this Act.

SEC. 106. AUTHORIZATION OF APPROPRIATIONS.

Amounts appropriated for operation of the historic site for each fiscal year after fiscal year 1994 may not exceed the amount appropriated for operation of the historic site for fiscal year 1994. No Federal funds may be expended at the site for purposes other than those specified in section 104 and in section 105(d). No funds may be appropriated after the enactment of this Act for any construction, development, or related activities with respect to the site without specific authorization by an Act of Congress.

TITLE II—DELAWARE WATER GAP NATIONAL RECREATION AREA

SEC. 201. BOUNDARIES.

Section 2(a) of the Act of September 1, 1965 (79 Stat. 612; 16 U.S.C. 460o–1(a)) establishing the Delaware Water Gap National Recreation Area is amended by striking "as generally depicted on the drawing entitled 'Proposed Tocks Island National Recreation Area' dated and numbered September 1962, NRA–TI–7100, which drawing is on file" and inserting "as generally depicted on the map entitled 'Delaware Water Gap National Recreation Area' dated November 1991 and numbered DWGNRA–620/80,900A' which shall be on file".

○

STATEMENT OF HON. BRUCE F. VENTO

Mr. VENTO. H.R. 3708 seeks to correct the longstanding and widely acknowledged problems of Steamtown's lack of authorization. In addition to establishing the site and its boundaries, the bill defines the limits of Steamtown's scope of activities, limits operating appropriations to current level and requires additional legislative authority for any future construction or development appropriation.

The bill is actually modeled after a measure that was worked out between myself and the principal sponsor of the bill, an advocate for Steamtown, Congressman McDade. There are some differences, but the initial authorization for Steamtown actually included all the operations and other activities which normally are not included in an authorization. They were, for whatever reason, in the initial authorization that was passed in 1986, and so now we are actually about four times over the amount of that authorization.

The subcommittee, of course, held hearings on this in 1991 based on reports from the GAO. Congressman McDade, who is with us today, introduced legislation, and at that time a version of that failed to be acted on. Unfortunately, I think we would have been far better off had we had that policy in place because there was a meeting of the minds at that point.

The basis of the compromise was that, in return for receiving funding to complete the somewhat scaled-back development of the site, Steamtown would operate pursuant to authorization and management requirements of the legislation. As it turned out, though, Steamtown received its appropriation and no authorization to guide it, whether by design or accident. The result is that this project continues to operate without appropriate legislative policy path and with no corrections of some of what I view as serious problems that have fueled the controversy with this site.

The measure before us today, while in itself controversial with some, takes the moderate course toward correcting Steamtown's lack of authorization. The bill moderates between those who would allow Steamtown to operate as it has in the past and continue its expansive sort of Byzantine growth and those who would deauthorize the site because of its cost and lack of historical integrity and significance.

In fact, as you know, last year there was an effort on the floor of the House to do just that, sort of a slam dunk. It isn't the sort of action that any of us would see as a reasoned deliberate policy path, and, of course, in the end it was not successful. It wouldn't be, certainly, my first priority, but, given no other options, it does represent a means of dealing with concern.

And I note that Congressman Andrews is submitting testimony. He had initially planned to testify, as well as other Members. Congressman Fawell is also submitting testimony.

I think, though, that I would like to put a positive tone on today's hearing, obviously trying to force the issue. The principal advocate, Congressman McDade, and I spoke earlier about reintroduction of a bill, and I think that, obviously, relations and views in that have been strained. So I think trying to get this hearing going and trying to get some positive dialog is important. It seems to me that today's testimony, which I have had a chance to review and I appreciate having it in advance, represents the range of perspectives about the future course of Steamtown.

This is an important issue which, of course, I treat very seriously, and I think that as we look at the modifications and the needs of the site, we are finding that there is a need to reach out and develop innovative means to deal with the operation and maintenance already there. And so I think the better path is, of course, to keep it as a unit but deal with these extraordinary costs that are attributed to the operation and the maintenance of the site.

In fact, I note that the Director in his testimony is asking for new authority under the 1935 Historic Sites Act which, apparently, they don't have right now which I understand that they would like to have to be able to deal with that particular problem.

I might point out to my colleague, Congressman McDade, specifically, that even the testimony from the Citizens Against Government Waste is in essence saying, yes, let's get a policy put in place with certain types of limits. It's unusual, but perhaps it's because of the unusual nature of this legislation.

So I think there is a basis to come to a meeting of the minds and work this out. Hopefully, then we can complete the loop and not have sort of the extraordinary effort on the floor of the House when we get to appropriations. But, in the absence of that, I cannot hold out to my colleague any type of solution. I think that it leads to that sort of confrontation and I think that would be a lot of energy and effort that doesn't take us to a conclusion with regard to this issue.

I am sure my colleague would like to get this on a regular path.

Mr. VENTO. With that said, let me say that all the statements of witnesses in their entirety, without objection, will be made a part of the record, and I am pleased to welcome my colleague, Congressman Joe McDade.

STATEMENT OF HON. JOSEPH M. McDADE

Mr. MCDADE. Thank you, Mr. Chairman. I appreciate the opportunity to testify today on H.R. 3708 and to report on the development of the Steamtown National Historic Site.

A great deal has happened at Steamtown since October 1991 when this subcommittee held hearings on reauthorization legislation. At that time, development of this historic site was 60 percent complete. Today, I am pleased to report that all of the planning and design is 100 percent complete, and the construction is just this side of 90 percent complete.

The historic roundhouse, the turntable, the education and visitor's center, the exhibit building, and the locomotive shop are all completed or nearing completion. The $66 million appropriated for development of Steamtown between fiscal years 1987 and 1993 is 99 percent obligated.

The project is on time and within budget. Planning is now underway for the official opening. We have been open to the public, but not officially. We hope to open officially to the public in July 1995.

The public has clearly been interested, the people whom we serve, in the story of American steam railroading that is told so magnificently at this historic site. I reported in 1991 that 130,000 people had visited the site. Two and a half years later that figure has grown to 677,000 total visitors. People have come from all 50 States and over 50 foreign countries. As many as 600,000 people are projected to visit the site annually once it has its official opening.

The excursion has been a huge success. Most trains have been sold out, 107,000 riders in 5 years of operation. More important than the numbers is the fact that visitors walk away with a greater knowledge and education of steam railroading and America's proud industrial heritage.

Steamtown does an excellent job of bringing to life this important chapter in our Nation's history. Visitors are able to see how a working steam locomotive rail yard operated in an earlier American era and envision that era of our industrial growth which was a critical period in the Nation's history.

Those of us who saw the potential of this site from the beginning are justifiably proud of Steamtown's development and excited about the future of this historic site.

Mr. Chairman, you have given permission, and I want to insert at this point in the record statements from the Governor of Pennsylvania in support, Gov. Robert P. Casey, a statement from former Gov. William W. Scranton in support, statements from Senators Arlen Specter and Harris Wofford, also supporting the project with your permission.

Mr. VENTO. Without objection, it will be added to the record.

[The prepared statements follow:]

UNITED STATES HOUSE OF REPRESENTATIVES
SUBCOMMITTEE ON NATIONAL PARKS, FORESTS AND PUBLIC LANDS
TESTIMONY OF PENNSYLVANIA GOVERNOR ROBERT P. CASEY
MAY 12, 1994

Mr. Chairman and other distinguished members of this subcommittee.

On behalf of 12 million Pennsylvanians, I want to thank you for this opportunity to offer comments in support of the Steamtown National Historic Site and to highlight its truly national and historic importance.

Steamtown is an impressive showcase for what became the second American revolution, our great industrial revolution in coal and iron and rail. It is a showcase that basically has been untouched by a century of change. Remarkably, the site itself was never plowed under or built over or consumed by the urban growth that has swallowed up so much of America's industrial past. That is why Steamtown doesn't just open a window on our past. It literally opens a door which we can all walk through and experience for ourselves the same sights and sounds and raw energy of 19th and early 20th century industrial development. And see it as most of us have never seen it before.

Steamtown will be able to offer the most advanced interpretation of a highly significant aspect of America's industrial heritage: an interpretation that the National Park Service has never been able to do before.

Steamtown is as much the story of the American people and the American worker as it is the story of industry and machinery. Because it was people -- the flood of immigrant workers who fired the furnaces and forged the rails and erected the giant locomotives -- who make the Steamtown story of yesterday worth showing and telling -- and retelling -- to the people of today and tomorrow. That's what Steamtown really is.

And the reason Steamtown is in Scranton is logical. Scranton is in the heart of Pennsylvania's Lackawanna Valley. It was here that our forefathers broke through the technological and industrial frontiers that America had to master before we could move beyond our rugged frontiers. Out of Scranton's furnaces and forges nearly a century-and-a-half ago came the first iron rails ever to be mass produced in the Western hemisphere. Iron rails from Steamtown that America's young railroads had to have if they were to fulfill their own westward destinies. Iron rails from Steamtown that were better, cheaper, and more accessible than any from England. In the process, as one noted historian has observed, Scranton became "the battleground where American Independence from English iron was fought and won." That victory on this industrial frontier is just as vital to the American experience as are the towering Sequoias and Grand Canyons of what was once our wild western frontier.

And it is absolutely proper and valid that this vital piece of our national heritage be preserved and interpreted for our people by the National Park Service, just as the Park Service interprets life at other points in our history, at other important sites in our history such as Independence Mall in Philadelphia; or the Lowell National Historic Park that interprets the old textile industry in Massachusetts; or Fort Union Trading Post that commemorates frontier life on the Missouri River; and just as Steamtown commemorates railroading and industrial life in the Lackawanna Valley of Pennsylvania.

Toward the end of the last century Scranton was seen as the energy boomtown of America, just as Dallas and Houston are in this century. Scranton was called the "Queen City of Anthracite" and the "Fireplace of the World." At one point as many as five rail lines converged on Steamtown, bringing in tens of thousands of workers and hauling away millions of tons of coal and the iron rails that carried the industrial revolution deep into America's heartland.

But the real significance of Steamtown's history rests with the people themselves. The Lackawanna Valley literally became a crucible of men and metal as immigrant families flocked there in search of the full promise of the emerging American industrial might. And under the fiery leadership of John Mitchell they fought oppression and spilled their blood to improve conditions for workers everywhere. Along the way, they built a community of bricks and mortar and -- perhaps more important -- spiritual strength that sustains the entire region today.

These were tough Americans, born in tough times, survivors of the toughest of tests. Their lives defined the American experience in microcosm. It's an experience that Steamtown, with your help, will bring alive for millions of domestic and foreign visitors in the years to come.

Now let's fast forward to the present, to the here and now, and talk about why it's important that Steamtown be allowed to interpret this wonderful history. The overriding reasons are commitment, investment, partnership and people.

First, commitment. My administration in state government has been committed to the successful development of the Steamtown National Historic Site from my first day on the job as Governor of Pennsylvania in 1987. Scranton is my hometown, and my hometown enthusiasm for Steamtown is obvious. These people are my people. My great-grandfather, my grandfather, and my father all started out in the coal mines near Steamtown. That's why the history we're talking about today is my history and why I'm so committed to its preservation.

Second, investment. Five years ago the Commonwealth of Pennsylvania launched an entirely new initiative established to preserve natural, cultural and recreational resources on a regional scale, and to enhance, manage and market these resources for tourism and economic development. We call it the Pennsylvania Heritage Parks Program.

As Governor of all of Pennsylvania, it has been my priority as well to devote public attention and resources to selected regions under the Heritage Parks Program where our cultural, historic and recreational assets exemplify the industrial traditions that have made our Commonwealth great and that Pennsylvania passed on to the rest of America. Steamtown epitomizes our industrial tradition, and that was a major factor in my decision to designate the Lackawanna Valley as Pennsylvania's first Heritage Park.

One of the early incentives for establishing this Heritage Parks Program was the commitment of the federal government to the restoration of The Steamtown National Historic Site. The excitement generated at the local level and the early partnership that developed demonstrated the need for opening the door to this part of America's history. From that early association with the National Site and the Park Service, we have designated five State Heritage Park regions. We have also designated three planning areas and one special study for a potential ninth Heritage Park.

To date, we have committed $7.5 million to the Heritage Parks Program which, in turn, will leverage at least $50 million from other sources.

And don't forget that Steamtown is unique in Park Service experience because all the land, all the equipment and even the buildings were donated to the federal government along with nearly $4 million from the City of Scranton and another $2.5 million in private donations.

Third, partnerships. Just like our steel, we in Pennsylvania know how to forge bonds of the highest integrity that will last a lifetime. Steamtown represents a new partnership among government at all levels and the private sector, joined in common cause to interpret the story of America's industrialization and railroads. To establish a framework for stewardship of our history and heritage, we've worked closely with the Park Service, the City of Scranton, the Steamtown Foundation and supporters from all across the country. We have all worked hard to put this partnership in place.

Finally, the most vivid reason of all why Steamtown should be allowed to succeed: people. People from all over, in bigger and bigger numbers. Steamtown has taken a page from that wonderful movie, Field of Dreams. You remember the words: "Build it and they will come." Visitors, volunteers, historians, scholars, train spotters and history buffs have come by the hundreds of thousands from every state in the nation and from more than 40 countries. And Steamtown is not even completed yet!

Every visitor, every day, validates Steamtown's historic relevance to the America of today and tomorrow. Visitor estimates keep going up by factors of a hundred thousand so that it now looks like Steamtown will attract as many as 600,000 people a year when all the work is done. And they will keep coming because Steamtown lets them step back in time so they can look and touch and realize the power that's in their lives from part of our history that's nearly been lost.

The people understand why Steamtown is important. They know that it was not the iron locomotives that came out of Steamtown's shops that make up our legacy. Instead, it was the character of the men and boys who built them. They know that it was not the iron rails that were produced there that made our people strong. Instead, it was the will of the people who forged them. They know that this is America's history, as raw-boned and uplifting as it gets. Their history. Our history. It is this legacy of character and will that compels Steamtown toward completion.

Thank you.

TESTIMONY OF FORMER GOVERNOR WILLIAM W. SCRANTON
MAY 12, 1994
THE SUBCOMMITTEE ON NATIONAL PARKS, FORESTS & PUBLIC LANDS
THE HONORABLE BRUCE F. VENTO, CHAIRMAN

The 19th century in America saw three major historical developments: the Civil War and the abolition of slavery, the opening of the American West, and the industrialization of the nation. The first two have received considerable attention, as they richly deserve, in the National Park system. The third, the industrialization of the nation, which created America's pre-eminence in the world, has been almost totally ignored except in splendid exhibits at stationary museums such as the Smithsonian. There is no working site demonstrating the development of America's industrial greatness. That is what makes Steamtown unique.

In the first chapter of Professor McPherson's remarkable one-volume history of the Civil War, he describes superbly the building of the vast railroad network achieved in 19th century America. That network was the stimulant, indeed the key to the dynamic industrialization of America.

Today Steamtown is the only site in the Eastern United States with the vestiges of the era of industrialization (1840 to 1920) in plain view -- and recoverable condition -- sixty-two acres in the middle of the downtown with car shops, locomotive shops, roundhouse, turntable, grand passenger station, a working yard, iron furnaces, passenger excursions -- and a restored coal mine nearby. There is no other site like it.

As the American rail network grew more coal was needed to power the steam engines. Then our industry graduated to steel and by the turn of the century America's industrialization had surpassed that of England, Germany or any other nation. That, all too briefly, is the story of 19th century American industrialization. It is also the story of Scranton -- railroads, iron furnaces, coal and steel from 1840 to 1920.

Uniquely, Scranton was the only city in the Northeast to develop precisely that way. The only one not to have water transportation by any means -- ocean, lake, river or canal. Railroads, five of them, shipped anthracite coal and powered Eastern America. Railroads made Scranton, and Scranton made rails and locomotives for the railroads. It truly was Steamtown! Night and day.

As William Penn Mott, the past Director of the National Park Service, stated Steamtown is "the ideal site" to offer education and recreation to Americans while they learn about, see and ride on our industrialized past and enjoy doing so.

Already, with the construction not yet completed, there have been four years of visitors and excursion riders, far more than anyone originally predicted. The expert prognosticators have had to re-assess their predictions -- first to 400,000 visitors per year, then to 500,000 and now to 600,000. Steamtown, still being restored and rebuilt, is already a success.

STEAMTOWN IS UNIQUE. THE ONLY SITE ANYWHERE WITH A WORLD-CLASS RAILROAD MUSEUM, AN OPERATING RAILROAD (with roundhouse, turntable, working railroad yard, mainline track), AND A HIGH-SPEED MAINLINE STEAM-POWERED EXCURSION. ALL ON AN HISTORIC RAILROAD SITE, paid for by the local community and donated to the National Park Service.

That brings me to what is the most important reason of all for the establishment of Steamtown. It is the story of people.

With the emergence of iron and steel and rails and railroads, immigrants arrived in America by the thousands and began their new lives with jobs in the mines, in the mills and on the railroads. These immigrants came from all over Europe -- English, Welsh, Scotch, Irish, Italian, German, Polish, Lithuanian, Slovaks and Slovenes, Russians -- altogether 42 different nationalities and ethnic groups to the Scranton area. All of them were enticed here by jobs in the mines, in the mills and on the railroads. These are the people who made Steamtown -- and in many cases gave their lives to it working in the mines and on the railroads.

George Washington did not sleep here. Abraham Lincoln never came here. But these people came by the thousands, and Steamtown as a result is the workingman's commemoration. It is a portrayal of industrial workers and their families.

Inextricably woven into this story of railroading and coal is the history of the American labor movement. It includes Terrence Powderly and John Mitchell. It recounts both abominable working conditions and bitter labor disputes as well as great achievements such as the enactment of the child labor laws and the eight-hour day.

The scale of railroading in Scranton and its necessary integration into coal mining and manufacturing created a prototype for business organization, labor relations, technology development and community formation in emerging industrial communities and post Civil War America. Our Heritage Valley Park demonstrates this to the utmost and Steamtown is the linchpin in that demonstration, the epitome of the early industrial revolution in America.

The sweat, toil and accomplishments of American industrial workers and American railroaders deserve a share of our resources. That is what Steamtown is all about.

Yes, it is for the nation. Yes, it will help the community which has suffered long and hard from unemployment and economic difficulties. Yes, it will cut the cost to the Federal and other governments by the drop in unemployment compensation and welfare payments in the area. But most of all, it is the true commemoration of what workers, mostly immigrants of 42 nationalities, accomplished in industrializing "the melting pot of the world", the United States of America.

Testimony of Senator Arlen Specter
Steamtown National Historic Site
May 12, 1994

Mr. Chairman, thank you for the opportunity to testify on an issue of great importance to Pennsylvania, the Steamtown National Historic Site. The continuation of the Steamtown National Historic Site is essential to maintain the unique place that steam locomotives hold in our nation's history.

The Steamtown project is intended to preserve and interpret elements of steam-operated railroads during the period of 1850 to 1950. The site currently consists of a 40-acre portion of the Delaware, Lackawanna and Western railyard located in downtown Scranton. The project calls for the restoration of the original locomotive repair shop from 1865, and for the construction of a new roundhouse, which will use the structure of the existing remnant roundhouse, originally built in 1902, to blend the old with the new. The roundhouse will enclose the working turntable, which will display 13 locomotives in an authentic environment. In addition, a 1926 Baldwin steam locomotive currently offers a 28-mile steam excursion from Scranton to Kingsley Station on the weekends.

Mr. Chairman, the citizens of Pennsylvania and railroad buffs alike are deeply grateful for Congress' past support for this project. These critically needed funds have been used to design the project and construct the Park Service's Steamtown headquarters and two museum buildings. When completed, the Steamtown National Historic Site will result in a blending of a railroad museum and a celebration of the Northeast's industrial heritage.

Aside from the historical and cultural significance of the Steamtown site, there is a valid economic basis for this project. Steamtown is at the core of the tourist industry marketing plan developed for the Lackawanna Heritage Valley by the Lackawanna Regional Planning Commission and the Greater Scranton Chamber of Commerce. The most recent Economic Impact and Visitor Profile, prepared by the Greater Scranton Area Chamber of Commerce and the National Park Service, shows that in 1993 the site had 156,749 visitors. These visitors spent well over $6 million in the area last year, and the total indirect economic impact of Steamtown National Historic Site was as much as approximately $40 million. Steamtown finished its fifth season with visitors from all 50 states and 38 countries, from as far away as Japan, New Zealand, and Argentina.

I would like to emphasize that the current plan for Steamtown is a scaled-back version of the original project. I believe that this reflects a balance between the wishes of the Authorizing Committee and the fiscal realities face by the Appropriations Committee. The National Park Service must be allowed to complete and operate Steamtown National Historical Site so that it can thoroughly educate and interpret the rich history of the industrial revolution and the part that railroads played in the development of American industrialism. I believe that Steamtown has clearly accomplished its goal of preserving history and has the added benefit of improving economic development within the boundaries established.

The railroad industry played a decisive role in transforming the United States from a vast, thinly populated agrarian country into the most powerful industrial nation on earth. Pennsylvania, and Lackawanna County in particular, are blessed with a fascinating history, having been in the midst of the industrial revolution. During the time period covered by the Steamtown museum, immigrants came from all over Europe to the Scranton area to find jobs in the mines, in the mills, and on the railroads. This exhibit brings to life a critical point in the history of this country's development for school children and other visitors who will visit the site.

Mr. Chairman, I ask that a letter from Mr. William Withuhn of the Smithsonian Institute be included in the Record. During the debate on Steamtown, it has been suggested that the Smithsonian Institute does not hold Steamtown in high regard. I believe the letter, Mr. Chairman, from Mr. Withuhn will address this misperception.

Mr. Chairman, I have been involved with this project since its inception, and I have visited Steamtown many times during my travels in Pennsylvania in the past several years. Many of my distinguished colleagues have testified on behalf of this worthwhile project, and I urge the House Committee to support Steamtown so the American people will have and enjoy an operational piece of the industrial revolution and American history.

NATIONAL MUSEUM OF AMERICAN HISTORY

SCIENCE, TECHNOLOGY, AND CULTURE

30 July 1993

The Honorable Arlen Specter
530 Hart Senate Office Building
United States Senate
Washington, DC 20510

Dear Senator Specter:

Thank you for your inquiry of July 29, 1993, in regard to the Steamtown National Historic Site of the National Park Service.

I have followed closely the progress of this National Historic Site since its initial legislation, for it involves my particular field of historic preservation. My opinions on Steamtown come from two distinct perspectives. First, as an historian and museum professional, I look at the site for its value to the American public as an historical legacy and, more importantly, as a place for the effective interpretation of that legacy. Secondly, as a former railroad manager and small business person, I look at the site in terms of its management, its costs, and especially its value-for-dollar to the public. If I may, therefore, I would like to respond to your request, and especially to your third paragraph, from the above perspectives.

I was an early critic of Steamtown. In my judgment, much of its early planning was poorly done. With respect to the early years that followed NHS designation, that still is my view.

Much has changed, however. During the last two years, and especially since last spring, I have spent considerable time at the site. The Park Service and its on-site staff have worked hard to respond to the early criticisms that came from various quarters, and they have taken a planning and management path that I find to be first-rate. I have examined the plans and proposed exhibits for the new visitor center now under construction, and I have become familiar with the daily operations of the site. In addition, I have had many opportunities to talk informally with visitors.

To summarize my views today, I believe Steamtown is a significant national asset and that its significance will increase. Steamtown will become one of the premier sites in the nation for the public interpretation of America's important industrial heritage. It will engage the public as no museum of static displays ever can.

Smithsonian Institution · Washington, D.C. 20560

The site will be, and is already, a place of living history. Visitors can see actual railroad operations, with real people operating and interpreting the pieces on view. And that is the point. The approach is fundamentally different from either a static museum or a tourist railroad. The former is focused on historic objects for their own sake; the latter is focused on giving tourists a pleasant ride, with no concern for conveying a sense of railroading as part of our nation's industry and history. Steamtown is a facility unique in North America, focused on the relationship of Americans to their industrial past, focused on working people and their roles in that legacy, and bringing an interpretation of this fully to life. When it is finished, in my view, the Steamtown National Historic Site will be a major step forward in helping Americans from all over the country understand the industrial heritage on which this country is built.

There has been controversy about the historic character of the site and its collections, but I think most of this discussion misses the point. Scranton is one of the few medium-sized cities in this country where there is a combination of historic railroad resources located close to center-city, and where the historic physical connections of railroad to city still exist. Certainly there are other places with more historic specimens, but nowhere else in the country is the combination of resources -- specimens, historic site, repair shops, heavy tools, a large urban station, and operational facilities -- as good for the interpretive mission of conveying what working life was like on the railroads.

The unique quality of the collections is that, for the most part, they are operable. The collection consists primarily of typical equipment from the "standard era" of steam railroading — locomotives, freight cars, and passenger cars. Their typicality is essential to the interpretive mission. In fact, it would be a serious mistake in my view to be operating unique, one-of-a-kind historical specimens -- those belong in museums in protected conditions. The Steamtown collection is one suited for operation -- and therefore, to me, of greater value to the goal of interpretation for the general public, as opposed to an audience of specialists.

As to costs, I believe that the public is being well served. Management of the planning process and of costs has been aggressive. Hard choices have been made as to what to preserve. The roundhouse/visitors center has been planned for maximum educational benefit, and from my museum management background, I believe the capital costs are reasonable. The operating costs, too, are reasonable and have been well thought out.

By and large, the US has been laggardly in preserving and interpreting its industrial history, compared to other countries. Great Britain, Germany, France, and even Switzerland, have outstanding industrial and railroad historic sites and living, operating museums. Internationally, the trend to living-history museums is well under way. Steamtown fits that trend. In this country, it has usually been unfashionable to celebrate working people and the industries in which they labored all their lives. Steamtown is helping redress the balance, in my view.

Visitors that I have talked to are enthusiastic in their reactions. They understand, I think, that Steamtown still looks rough around the edges. Amenities are few at this point, because the site is under construction. But already the interim operations are well received. And the high-quality interpretation, by experienced park rangers and guides, already adds greatly to the overall visitor experience. Visitation from around the country, I believe, will rapidly increase once the site is fully open and functioning.

"Functioning" is a fundamental part of the whole. The investment in the site can be rendered meaningless by unwise cuts in its operations. Care in budgeting is always essential. I believe the Park Service has exercised that care. I would urge those who are concerned to study the site and its operations, as I have, to better evaluate the cost/benefit in the interests of the public. A cut of operating funds at this juncture would be disastrous, in my view; Steamtown would then simply revert to being just another static industrial museum. The heart would then be cut out of its essential character and unique value to the American public.

Sincerely,

Wm. L. Withuhn

William L. Withuhn
Curator of Transportation

cc: Senator Harris Wofford

Written Testimony Of Senator Harris Wofford
Steamtown Reauthorization Bill
U.S. House of Representatives
Subcommittee on National Parks, Forests,
and Public Lands
May 12, 1994

Mr. Chairman. Members of the committee. I want to thank you for providing me the opportunity to submit a statement for the record in support of the National Railroad Museum at Steamtown.

Most railroad museums in the United States are displayed as a static collection, where nothing moves, nothing works like a real railroad yard. By contrast, Steamtown is a site that has been home to the Delaware, Lackawanna, and Western Railroad for over one hundred and thirty years. It is a site that is listed on the National Register of Historic Places because of its leading role in our nation's industrial and economic development.

Steamtown enjoys broad bi-partisan support from the public and private sector. In 1992, then-Secretary of the Interior Manuel Lujan toured the park and declared that it was "the real thing...I can see the potential". William Withuhn, Curator of Transportation for the Smithsonian Institution and an early critic of Steamtown, wrote to me on August 3, 1993 to say that after spending considerable time at the site, he concluded that Steamtown is a significant national asset and that its

86-965 - 95 - 2

significance will increase with time. "Steamtown will become one of the premier sites in the nation for the public interpretation of America's important industrial heritage," he wrote. "It will engage the public as no museum of static display ever can." National Park Service Director, Roger G. Kennedy, last month visited Steamtown to lend his support for the site. Mr. Kennedy concluded that not all national parks are places of zoos or of waterfalls. Instead, he said there are parks such as Ellis Island, Independence Hall, and Steamtown. "This is one place in America where actual life is represented...It contains the American experience," he noted.

What is most important for you to know is the depth of support for Steamtown that has come from the state and local level. The Commonwealth of Pennsylvania, the local government, and the private sector have contributed some $20 million to this project. No federal funds have been used for land acquisition. The forty acres of land, the collection of twenty-nine steam locomotives, eighty-two period rail cars, the equipment, and the great majority of the total collection of over one million pieces have all been donated to the National Park Service.

In addition, the community knows that money in and of itself is not the answer to Steamtown's success. Last year alone volunteers contributed over 17,000 hours of work to Steamtown. Some served on the train and engine crews as engineers, firefighters, and conductors. Some volunteered as tour guides or worked with the curator on logging archival material. Still others helped repair and maintain the locomotives and cars.

The Steamtown Volunteer Association, a non-profit support group of the park, has contributed over seventy thousand hours to the park since 1988. These volunteers have saved the National Park Service the equivalent of $1,193,340 in salaries. As someone who has been a longtime advocate of voluntary national service, I am especially pleased to see Steamtown become such a magnet for this kind of active duty citizenship and service.

Finally I want to make the point that the greatest waste of all would be to fail to finish the job that has been started at Steamtown. According to the Park Service, the project is about eighty-five percent completed. For the taxpayers to see the return on the investment that has already been made, we should make the commitment to taking the last few steps. It would be a shame for a young person to invest and work for three years in college and never finish the degree that would bring so many new benefits and opportunities in life. It does not make sense for us not to see our country realize the educational, cultural, and economic benefits of a thriving Steamtown.

Mr. McDADE. They were unable to be here, but they all wanted, Mr. Chairman, the opportunity to share their insights on the significance of Steamtown. They eloquently point out the unique ability of this historic site as the Nation's only operating railroad museum to commemorate and interpret the story of the Nation's railroads and the people who built and operated them.

We are particularly proud of the high levels of volunteerism that occur at the Steamtown historic site—we have one of the highest volunteer levels in the system. And, equally significant is the $14.5 million in funds and donations that have come into the system from non-Federal sources. This will be addressed a bit later in the morning by the Honorable Mr. Angeli, who serves in Governor Casey's cabinet as secretary of the Pennsylvania Department of Community Affairs, and I am happy that he is with us here this morning.

Mr. Chairman, I do want to take a moment to thank Mayor Jim Connors who drove most of the night to be present in the hearing room to be of whatever assistance he could be. He spent the night on the highway to get here. He has a statement which I would like to submit for the record, and I want to publicly thank him for going a lot of extra miles through the dark of night to be here to testify at this important hearing. I am very grateful to him.

Mr. VENTO. Is there some misunderstanding about whether or not he was going to be on the agenda?

Mr. McDADE. Yes. There was originally a statement that he could testify and then there was some talk about——

Mr. VENTO. We would be happy to hear from him, I think.

Mr. McDADE. Thank you, Mr. Chairman, I appreciate that. If time constrains, he has a statement.

Mr. VENTO. He is on the witness list. I was told that he has always been on the witness list. But we will be hearing from him personally, and his statement will be part of the record.

Mr. McDADE. I want to go back to the hearing in 1991 and some of the problems that were addressed at that time in the hearing:

I want to point out that 100 percent of the EPA-mandated remediation of hazardous wastes has been completed. There are no hazardous wastes at the site.

All of the key properties have been acquired by donation, Mr. Chairman, with no additional expense to the Park Service.

All track and bridge repairs are successfully completed.

A long-term cooperative agreement with the Lackawanna County Rail Authority for maintenance and use of the tracks is negotiated and in place.

In 1993, Mr. Chairman, the revenues charged for the excursion have covered total expenses, and the safety record, Mr. Chairman, has been exemplary. More than 5.5 million passenger miles have been traveled without a problem.

One thing that has not changed is the historic significance of Steamtown. The entire site has been placed on the National Register of Historic Places as being nationally significant for its role in the development of steam railroad transportation during the industrial revolution.

When Steamtown was originally authorized in 1986, William Penn Mott, then the Director of the Park Service, and Public Lands

Subcommittee Chairman John Seiberling were enthusiastic about the project and convinced of its historic importance. Mr. Mott called Steamtown a "national historic treasure." And Congressman Seiberling said Steamtown offers a way for the—and I am quoting John now—"history of the railroad to be preserved and interpreted for present and future generations."

Mr. Chairman, I want to commend the National Park Service for the excellent job they do. I have been privileged to be on the Interior Subcommittee of Appropriations for 30 years. I have taken a great interest in the National Park Service, as has my friend from Minnesota. I have seen them, in the main, do superb work, and I think they have done that here.

Steamtown's efforts to interpret and present to the public the era of 1890 to 1950 in our industrial heritage is going superbly. We don't get negative comments from the people who come in to visit the site. All we get is positive applause that it is there for them to see, to take their children to see, to smell, to watch, to understand and to enlarge their knowledge as no other static museum is able to do that deals with the question of railroading in the United States.

Mr. Chairman, I commend you for your initiative in drafting legislation, and I want to see a reauthorization bill move forward. But, I must express my concerns about the micromanagement features of the bill which will, in my view, impede the Park Service from effectively managing this site.

I am particularly concerned about restrictions that have been placed on the number of locomotives that may be restored and restrictions on excursion operations. If I could just try to highlight that for you, Mr. Chairman.

As you know, the current legislation has a 50-mile limit and a limit on the number of steam locomotives that can be operated. In effect, Mr. Chairman, it takes flexibility away from the superintendent who feels that the excursions are a useful interpretive tool. And, these restrictions also have financial consequences.

What do I mean by that? What I mean is to go on the current excursion you have to fire up a train, which is a major expense. Once it is ready it can do a multiplicity of jobs, and it doesn't have to be refired. You spent the money up front.

And that is what you must do with this particular kind of machine, so that, Mr. Chairman, if the Canadian Pacific, which now owns a mainline directly into the Steamtown yards all the way to Canada, said we want to run an excursion to Canada and we are prepared to give x number of dollars to underwrite it and you charge $400 a seat, you could keep the income. We would make several hundred thousand dollars of income into the site to defray operational costs and to ameliorate the squeeze that all the parks are experiencing.

Mr. Chairman, in my view, it is essential for the Superintendent to have the flexibility he needs to manage the historic site efficiently and effectively.

The greatest concern you have, that I have and you know I have spoken to you about, is this cap on operational dollars. Mr. Chairman, I just cannot in any way endorse this provision. I think that it is a mistake to interfere with the normal budget process that goes on from the time a superintendent assesses his needs, negotiates those needs through the OMB process, and ultimately becomes part of the President's budget which is submitted to the Congress each year.

And, finally, the people's representatives then have the opportunity to make the final disposition of whatever that proposal is, based, we hope, always on public need. That is what you and I attempt to do as we serve our constituencies.

So I would hope, Mr. Chairman, you are able to rethink that provision and look at it from the standpoint of permitting the normal budget process to continue to work as it always has. Let the NPS do its scrubbing at OMB and present to us, as the people's representative, an administration which we will consider in Congress. Mr. Chairman, I am committed to finding common ground that will meet the needs of the American public.

Mr. Chairman, I am grateful for the opportunity to appear before you, and I appreciate your many courtesies.

Mr. VENTO. Well, thank you, Congressman McDade.

[Prepared statement of Mr. McDade follows:]

Statement of

CONGRESSMAN JOSEPH M. MCDADE

May 12, 1994

SUBCOMMITTEE ON NATIONAL PARKS AND PUBLIC LANDS

Mr. Chairman, Members of the Subcommittee, I welcome and appreciate the opportunity to testify today on H.R. 3708 and to report on the progress and development of the Steamtown National Historic Site.

A great deal has happened at Steamtown since October of 1991 when this Subcommittee held hearings on reauthorization legislation. At that time, development of this historic site was 60 percent complete. Today, I am pleased to report that all of the planning and design is 100 percent complete and construction is 86 percent complete. The historic roundhouse and turntable, the education and visitor's center, exhibit building and the locomotive shop are all completed or nearing completion. The $66 million appropriated for development of Steamtown between fiscal years 1987 and 1993 is 99 percent obligated.

The project is on time and within budget. Planning is now underway for the official grand opening in July of 1995.

The public has clearly been interested in the story of American steam railroading that is told so magnificently at this historic site. I reported to the Subcommittee in 1991 that 130,000 people had visited the site. Two and a half years later, that figure has grown to 677,000 total visitors. People have come from all 50 states and over 50 foreign countries. As many as 600,000 people are projected to visit the site annually once it officially opens.

The excursion has been a great success, with over 107,000 rides in its five years of operation. Steamtown has operated about five and a half million accident-free excursion passenger miles since 1989.

More important than the numbers is the fact that visitors walk away from the site with a greater knowledge of steam railroading and America's industrial heritage. Steamtown does an excellent job of bringing to life this important chapter in our nation's history. Visitors are able to see how a working steam locomotive railyard operated in an earlier American era which saw tremendous industrial growth and the dominance of rail as a form of transportation.

Those of us who saw the potential of this site from the beginning are justifiably proud of Steamtown's development and excited about the future of this historic site. At this time, I would like to submit for the hearing record the statements of four distinguished Pennsylvanians who are very familiar with and have been instrumental to the development of Steamtown.

The statements are from Robert Casey, Governor of the Commonwealth of Pennsylvania, former Governor William Scranton and United States Senators Arlen Specter and Harris Wofford. They were unable to be here but they all wanted the opportunity to share their insights on the significance of Steamtown. They eloquently point out the unique ability of this historic site, as the nation's only operating railroad museum, to commemorate and interpret the story of the nation's railroads and the people who built and operated them.

We are particularly proud of the high levels of volunteerism and the over $14.5 million in funds and donations from non-Park Service sources. Later you will hear from Ray Angeli, who serves on Governor Casey's Cabinet as Secretary of the Pennsylvania Department of Community Affairs. Secretary Angeli will elaborate on the local and state involvement. I look forward to his testimony, as I know you do, Mr. Chairman.

I am also pleased that Scranton Mayor Jimmy Connors is here today. As a former history teacher and two-term Mayor, he can speak volumes about the historic value of Steamtown and the local commitment that has been made and continues to be made. I want to acknowledge him at this time and submit his written statement for the hearing record.

Some of the problems of concern to this Subcommittee at the 1991 hearing have been addressed:

--One hundred percent of the EPA-mandated remediation of hazardous wastes have been completed.

-- All of the key properties have been acquired by donation.

-- All track and bridge repairs have been successfully completed.

-- A long-term cooperative agreement with the Lackawanna County Rail Authority for maintenance and use of the tracks has been negotiated.

-- The revenues charged for the excursion have covered total expenses, and the safety record has been exemplary.

One thing that has not changed is the historical significance of Steamtown. The entire site has been placed on the National Register of Historic Places as being nationally significant for its role in the development of steam railroad transportation during the Industrial Revolution. It should be remembered that 21 years ago the National Park Service initiated and conducted a new area study which concluded that Lackawanna Valley possesses national historical significance and should be a unit of the Park Service System.

When Steamtown was originally authorized by the House, William Penn Mott, and Public Lands Subcommittee Chairman John Seiberling were enthusiastic about the project and convinced of its historic importance. Mr. Mott called Steamtown a national historic treasure, and Congressman Seiberling said Steamtown offers a way for the "history of the railroad in the United States to be preserved and interpreted for present and future generation."

Mr. Chairman, I want to take this opportunity to correct a common misconception about Steamtown. Earlier this week it was reported as fact by one of the Congressional reports that no hearings were ever held on Steamtown before the original appropriation was made. This is untrue, as you know. The Public Land Subcommittee held a hearing on September 30, 1986, and the House passed authorizing legislation on October 6 of that same year.

Returning to the historical significance of the site, it should be noted that the Steamtown Comprehensive Management Plan, which was signed by Interior Secretary Manuel Lujan and Park Service Director James Ridenour, points out that "the Steamtown site and collection represents topics or themes in the National Park System Plan that are worthy of commemoration and currently unrepresented or underrepresented."

I want to commend the Park Service for the excellent job that has been done to make the Steamtown site an enjoyable, safe and educational place to visit and for carrying out the intent of Congress to preserve and interpret the role of steam-operated railroads during the period of 1850 to 1950.

I was delighted that Park Service Director Roger Kennedy was able to visit Steamtown last month. He's here today to offer his personal observations. I was pleased that he praised the site as a living park of international importance which offers an effective venue to learn about the past. He described the site in the same context as Independence Hall and Ellis Island in that it represents the experience of people rather than the preservation of a natural resource.

Mr. Kennedy will address some of the specifics of H.R. 3708 from the Park Service perspective. I know his comments will certainly merit our attention.

One of the matters which he may address is a proposed Educational Partnership with the University of Scranton. This proposal will allow the Site to be operated at considerable savings to the federal government and can serve as a pilot project for possible application at other units of the Park Service.

The partnership will enable the University to operate the Core Complex of the Park by offering visitor, custodial and management services. The University would collect a program fee from visitors.

Both the Park Service and the University would benefit. The partnership would reduce future staffing and alleviate the burden of utility bills and custodial services at the Core Complex. The University will develop an educational laboratory that will be linked to its Business Leadership Program and managed by the Center for Public Initiatives.

Mr. Chairman, I commend you for your initiative in drafting legislation, and I want to see the reauthorization move forward. I am very concerned, however, about some of the micromanagement features of the bill which will, in my view, counterproductively impede the Park Service from having the flexibility needed to effectively manage the site. I am particularly concerned about restrictions that would be placed on the number of locomotives which may be restored and operated and the restrictions on excursion operations.

Of greatest concern to me, however, is the provision to freeze annual operating funds at the fiscal year 1994 level. This is an unprecedented action which would undermine the investment made by Congress on behalf of the American people. Operations of all units of the National Park System should depend on the public needs and priorities as determined by the people's elected representatives in Congress, and not on statutory limits. The Administration's budget recommendations should be a guide as we make those decisions each year.

Mr. Chairman, we share a tremendous interest in the future of our national parks and historic sites. I served for years as Ranking Republican on the Interior Appropriations Subcommittee and still serve on that panel. We have worked hand in hand with the authorizing committee over the years to develop the National Park System. I am proud, as I know you are, of what we have accomplished.

I have visited a great many of the parks that the Congress has funded, and I am always impressed by the contribution they make to our nation. It's a legacy we pass on to our children and grandchildren which will last long after we are gone.

I have great confidence in the National Park Service to manage these sites in a responsible and cost-efficient manner. We should not restrict their flexibility or tie the hands of Congress when we act each year on the Administration's recommendations. I do not think we should take away our ability to do our job, at Steamtown National Historic Site, or anywhere else with an inflexible freeze on operations levels. It is an unprecedented move, which I hope you will reconsider.

Thank you for providing me this opportunity to comment on this legislation and the progress of Steamtown. I look forward to the hearing today and to working with you to develop a reauthorization bill that will allow Congress and the Park Service to carry out its responsibilities.

Mr. VENTO. Obviously, this is a very important issue, and it has obviously caused a great deal of concern on your part as the GAO reports and the events have occurred, sometimes in terms of reaction, unfortunately, not being proactive. So my better side, and I think all of our better sides, are being proactive on some of these issues which we tried to do in 1991.

We came very close to an agreement, and I think if we had done that we wouldn't be here today. We wouldn't have some of the acrimony that has occurred over the past few years. So it is the effort here to try to get this out before we get to the confrontative stage which could very well happen again unless there is agreement.

Mr. MCDADE. We appreciate the opportunity to talk with you, Mr. Chairman, and try to come to an agreement here.

Mr. VENTO. Well, I think the focus of this has been helpful. In fact, there have been a number of events that have occurred in recent months.

You know, the basic issue right now that is outstanding is the concern the Park Service has about the advisory committee. I have generally not been favorably disposed and have tried to discourage commissions and advisory groups where they are not necessary, sort of the reinvention of the political subdivision. It shouldn't be our role. I think accountability gets somewhat foggy in that process, and you really have to justify needing one.

In this case, I think there is some logic in terms of having an advisory committee. Congressman McDade, you know, working on park issues for 30 years, and you have done a great job and have been a great advocate and ally with regards to a lot of issues—but this is extraordinary in terms of the size and scope of what has happened here. There has been, as you know, my challenge with regard to the basic fabric versus the reconstruction of sites, and I think it is always, I suppose, an area where you would say there is a gray area; but there has been a heck of a lot of reconstruction on this particular site, and you recognize that, I am certain.

Mr. MCDADE. Well, Mr. Chairman, I don't think it is that sort of an unusual process, however. Lowell and Salem have gone through this same sort of an operation, and I don't think we are that much different from either side. The Presidio, which is the newest unit, has all sorts of ramifications to it that we are beginning to sort through and try to find out because I think we all want to see that property preserved, and we don't know where that is going to play out.

As we go back and forth, we have to come to grips with what part of the past should be preserved and how to balance those sometimes clashing interests.

But, Mr. Chairman, on the advisory committee, may I say to you that when I originally sat down in those days, it was John Seiberling, Chairman of the Public Lands Committee, and Ron Marlenee, the ranking member, and together with their staffs we crafted the legislation which became the first Steamtown authorization bill that was passed unanimously in the House. We intended at that time to try to put in an advisory committee. We felt that that would be a very useful thing, and it would be a mechanism by which we could reach out to people of all stripes around the country and get them to focus and dialogue on the issue of how we should do this even better.

We encountered the same problem you are describing. OMB said no. Since the original authorization, we have developed a voluntary group, totally unpaid, totally unreimbursed for expenditures, which meets and gives advice about what ought to happen with respect to the park. That volunteer group has been a great help to the superintendent and to me as a sounding board to meet and try to discuss policy, so we kind of—as Yogi Berra would say, it is deja vu all over again with respect to that question.

Mr. VENTO. Let me take the major issue. You may have to be on your way. Of course, you are invited to sit in on this and hear the other witnesses if your schedule permits, but I certainly understand, if your schedule is anything like mine, that it may not be possible.

But the issue of the operation and maintenance type of annual funding issue—incidentally, I was surprised to find out when advised that the initial legislation had, in fact, included this in its cap.

Mr. MCDADE. I tried to put it in at that time.

Mr. VENTO. But it obviously means that the issue is actually sort of outstanding. But it is unusual——

Mr. MCDADE. It is for the same reason, OMB's objection.

Mr. VENTO. Right. But I am sure we could find some agreement on that. We are after getting something practical. Obviously, the maintenance and operation expenses here are, to say the least, very, very unusual in terms of the cost of operating.

Mr. MCDADE. They are about the same as Lowell Historic Site, may I say to my friend, and we are well down the list from the Presidio, which is your No. 1 operational impact now and the newest addition to the WPS. We are well down from that.

Mr. VENTO. One of the things that has come up, Congressman McDade, is the issue of this partnership. I think the point is there is a recognition as you go fully operational that the costs will be substantial. And there is, obviously, a lot of pressure on the Appropriations Committee. The fact is there are efforts to try and reduce or limit what the operating expense would be and maintenance expense. It isn't exactly something that is unaddressed or unrecognized by the principals that are working on the proposal.

So your suggestion is if we were to grant authority to do certain activities in terms of fees or do other things to reduce the cost, then in that context with the authority which you do not now have—at least I don't think you do, but that may be an arguable point—but the point is, isn't there something we could work out in terms of dealing with that and then at another time limit what the exposure would be in terms of operating and maintenance?

In other words, if we grant one authority to pick up revenue from another source to enable and fulfill what the goal is, the operational costs, that sets a factor. And I listened with special interest to your discussion about the special excursions that might, in fact, substantially reduce costs, and we might be able——

I think what we are concerned about here is that if we have long excursions that result in heavier and heavier types of subsidies and operating expenditures and loss, most people that walk into a park end up costing us more than they deliver in terms of a fee. But that is OK. That is how it is. Nobody expects that if it costs $20 a visitor to go to, for example, to Tumacacori in southern Arizona, so be it.

But the point is we have a responsibility in terms of the stewardship. Maybe they pay a fee for a few bucks and it costs us that, but we have a responsibility in terms of keeping it reasonable.

But what I am trying to do is talk about some mixture of components here, one which you are trying to assess—not a user fee. I am trying to think of the phrase. It isn't an entrance fee.

Mr. McDADE. It is a program fee.

Mr. VENTO. A program fee which is automatically permitted to be expended, doesn't have to go back through the awful appropriations process and OMB process, so that it stays within the park. It is unusual, this permit or program fee that you call it.

Mr. McDADE. Well, you know, that is a decision that was made at the highest levels of the department and the Park Service, and I would defer to Director Kennedy to respond to that.

Mr. VENTO. No, I am just suggesting to you the mixture. We are not there yet, either. And I don't know what they think they can do or what you think, but my point is that if we, in other words, legislatively can mix that together, we might be able to work out a limitation. There is a recognition.

All I am trying to suggest to you is this view in terms of the operation and maintenance challenge.

Mr. McDADE. Mr. Chairman, I want to say that one of the things that we worked out back with John Seiberling, Ron Marlenee and the staff, was the inclusion of the Historic Sites Act. It is in the bill and one of the authorities under which we operate. We want to keep that because we believe it has broader authorities, legislatively granted, but I will let the Director address that question.

Mr. VENTO. No, he can, fine. They have some explanation of authorities under that that have never been utilized which are completely unique. So I am just suggesting to you that, based on the fact that it is 60 years old, I don't know what the legislative intent was, so that is, I think, rather a precarious type of existence. But I think we could probably do something to reinforce this.

If we are going to act on legislation and if you are going to accept certain types of limitations, we could probably be explicit with regards to that because the end result would be the same in terms of helping offset the operation and maintenance expenditure, achieving the objective of a revenue flow on operation and maintenance, and satisfying or at least giving us some certainty and predictability, that we would not have. It would also then permit a liberalization, as you say, or talk about some of the excursion issues that might be on a special basis where they could be completely funded by the other sources outside of the Park Service.

See, one of the limits we have here is the 25 percent cap that we had talked about before.

Mr. McDADE. Mr. Chairman, in 1993, and since then, the excursion run has been self-liquidating. There was no cost. And that is a monument to management, in my opinion, because my experience is probably like yours, that if you are involved in mass transportation it is a losing venture.

Mr. VENTO. That is right.

Mr. MCDADE. But some of the things they get approached about involve the special excursions, fall foliage for instance.

About 40 minutes away from this site is the largest single concrete viaduct bridge in the world, modeled after the Roman aqueduct in Nimes, France. There are people who are enamored of the thought of just being able to go across that bridge, fall foliage, spring foliage, summertime, whatever, take their photographs, see the incredible panorama that unfolds from this bridge. And that is something that we would like to be able to think about in terms of the public experiences because the creation of that bridge in the railroading history of the country is a story all to itself. It is on the Historic Registry, of course, and it is a story worth telling itself, but if you can't get to it in any kind of a reasonable way, you know, it is just off the bounds.

So we would like to be able to have flexibility to talk about such issues, let the Park Service, through its interpretive and educational programs, make an effort to see how they deal with those issues rather than have a blanket prohibition imposed.

Mr. VENTO. The concern, of course, that I have is principally the operation and maintenance. If you just expand this to beyond no limitations—I mean, at least we have park boundaries. We have other factors. But when we get into the transportation issue, the railroad tracks of America would be the limit.

Mr. MCDADE. What is wrong with that? I mean, if it doesn't cost the National Park Service?

Mr. VENTO. If there were no exposure or operation and maintenance expenditure to the Park Service by virtue of this, other than whatever they have in terms of the rolling stock authority that might be traveling, then I think that satisfies a major concern. If we can do that through fees—and the same is true of onsite type of expenditures which we are talking about in terms of a program fee or a permit fee. Actually, the law provides for three types of fees under the Historic Sites Act, which, of course, is a completely new authority that has never been utilized to date, according to the legal memo from Mr. Conte.

Mr. MCDADE. That was the reason, Mr. Chairman, that John Seiberling and Ron Marlenee suggested we incorporate it into the act since we were trying to do an historic interpretation.

Mr. VENTO. I know there was a hearing on this issue, and there have been suggestions on how to resolve this. The provision was authorized through the appropriations process and Mr. Seiberling's and Mr. Marlenee's involvement.

Mr. MCDADE. Mr. Chairman, just to correct the record on that. What happened was there was a hearing in front of the Public Lands Subcommittee of this committee. It was referred to the full committee and unanimously put on the suspense calendar, passed by the House without dissenting vote. Then, when we got to the end of the session, the Senate, as we have already talked about, couldn't find room on its calendar, and it was folded into the continuing resolution.

So the exact language that passed the House back in the early 1980's is what was enacted into the continuing resolution. It was

House-drafted language which unanimously passed the U.S. House of Representatives.

Mr. VENTO. Well, I understand what happened. But the concern, of course, has been that now there is not authorization for the total amount of work that was done and, consequently, that is of concern. The dollars were appropriated well beyond what the ceiling was in that 1986 bill, and, of course, the efforts to authorize have not been successful.

The concern, of course, is that we don't want the Park Service to be taking care of the repair, maintenance and operation of that trackage all over America, as in the case of the excursion that now pays for itself.

Mr. MCDADE. There is surely no contemplation that we are going to replace or repair trackage areas across America.

Mr. VENTO. I understand, but we have repaired all 13 miles or at least have contributed substantially to 13 miles of private rail line that is now being maintained. Obviously, if there was money to be made in running railroads they would still be running in a lot of our communities.

I know my State of Minnesota had one of the most extensive trackage of any State in the Nation. Some of it, in fact, bringing in coal probably from Pennsylvania before the——

Mr. MCDADE. I wouldn't be surprised.

Mr. VENTO. Which I was reminded of by some of your advocates here. In any case, we have abandoned a lot of lines.

Mr. MCDADE. We have in Pennsylvania as well.

Mr. VENTO. In fact, we use them now for bicycle paths.

In any case, I won't hold you, but you know I wanted to state my interest to you. Unfortunately, this is sort of a public forum to do it, but, in any case, I think that you and I would talk candidly in private at will.

I think everything is pretty much right on the table with me in terms of this issue. You know my concerns, and I raise them with regards to the re-creation and reconstruction versus the historic fabric. I think it is a problem, and it is a question of how far you go, how much you need in terms of interpretation.

Those decisions have been made pragmatically. I can't go back and change them. But I think there were debates there that should have taken place and reviewed more carefully, but they are there. The concern now is to get this on a path where we can reduce the obligations and responsibilities. This thing has to go beyond our service around here.

Mr. MCDADE. Indeed, Mr. Chairman, this is in perpetuity.

Mr. VENTO. The point is we want to see this so we have a sound policy to take that forward. I know how proud you are of it, the people indicated there by the two governors' position and others. We just have to get agreement and get this thing done. I will be working toward that end, and I look forward to your involvement.

Mr. MCDADE. Mr. Chairman, I appreciate that. I have to be at the Appropriations Committee at 11:30. David Obey and I have reached an agreement on the allocation of the 602. We are going to present it to the full Appropriations Committee, but I would like to remain for a while if I may.

Mr. VENTO. Sure.

Mr. Dickey, you didn't have any questions of our colleague, did you? You just came in.

Mr. DICKEY. No, sir.

Mr. VENTO. I would be pleased to have you join me at the committee table.

Let me ask the Director of the Park Service, Mr. Roger Kennedy, to present his testimony. He is accompanied by Dr. John Latschar, who is the Superintendent of Steamtown National Historic Site.

STATEMENT OF ROGER KENNEDY, DIRECTOR, NATIONAL PARK SERVICE, DEPARTMENT OF THE INTERIOR, ACCOMPANIED BY JOHN A. LATSCHAR, SUPERINTENDENT, STEAMTOWN NATIONAL HISTORIC SITE

Mr. KENNEDY. Mr. Chairman, we have submitted formal testimony.

Mr. VENTO. Yes, it has been made part of the record, Mr. Director. Welcome.

Mr. KENNEDY. Thank you. Just a couple of informal comments.

This is and has been a rambunctious horse, which comes to mind more than an engine. We concur with the view that you have eloquently stated that it needs a bridle. We don't think it ought to be shot.

We support vigorously the constraints that you have offered in your bill. We have, as you know, as we always do, some suggestions of our own, but they don't go to any of the fundamentals of the proposal before us.

It is clear that there is now a unit of the National Park System which does something that no other unit does. It is a living process that manifests the industrial process and really not just railroad history; in a very tangible way, something that no museum in America does, either.

I think, however, for me the most telling reality of this project in its current condition is that it is now embedded in the life of this community. It is not an isolated park unit. It is really the core of the city of Scranton's sense of its own history, and it pulls together a community which has had the usual tensions of an industrial town.

It is now rather pretty in many ways, but it has shown the history of the tensions in American social life in violent and in powerful, emotional ways. And the life of the railroaders, people who work on trains, who made the trains, made them run, managed them, is manifested in a daily way that makes it possible for generations to communicate with each other about that experience.

It is entirely true that that could have been done behind the Great Northern Depot in St. Paul, MN. It has been done in Scranton, PA. It exists, and as you suggested earlier and Mr. McDade has, the question essentially before us is how do we make maximum use of this existing facility which provides a service to the Nation within constraints that can assure us that tensions and difficulties that have beset its creation will not recur in the future.

In particular, Mr. Chairman, you referred to what is absolutely an unusual way of compensating for the annual operating expenses. The people of this community, with the resourceful assistance of an intelligent and resourceful superintendent, have come up with a way to pick up about 40 percent or so of what it is going to cost to run the place every year by charging what is essentially a fee for the use of a part of the premises.

Clearly, the law, the Land and Water Conservation Act itself, prohibits the charging of fees for visitors' centers. It does not prevent and I assume, since I think you wrote this provision, it wasn't intended to prevent access once people got into parks. It wasn't intended to prevent the people who use parks from paying for such specialized facilities as theaters or museums and things of that sort.

Mr. VENTO. If I could interrupt you, I think that, furthermore, that the law forbids volunteers from collecting fees, in other words, anything other than the Park Service personnel in terms of collecting fees, which is another complication that faces you, Mr. Director.

Mr. KENNEDY. Yes, it does, sir, and I want to assure you that the recency of this resourceful device leads me to express to you a desire to—first of all, we are not going to use any such process until we have thoroughly discussed it with you and your staff. I think we need all of you to understand precisely how we will thread our way to the objective of having this be a self-supporting enterprise to the extent that that is possible and at the same time accommodate all provisions of law and the intention of those laws at the same time. We are not going to go forward with this program until we have had an adequate opportunity to discuss it with you.

With regard to another matter that you and Mr. McDade referred to which has to do with the relationship of the legislation of 1986 which essentially gave pretty full scope to cooperative agreements, one could either recur to the language of the 1986 act or we could simply stipulate perhaps—you could stipulate perhaps at the top that this proposal—proposed set of reforms would be within the authority of the Historic Sites Act which would do essentially the same thing. Either would give a kind of breadth to provide for cooperative agreements between the park itself and such institutions as the University of Scranton and other friends' groups.

It is true that, while we got here in an unusual way, the people of this community have certainly demonstrated a vigorous desire to recognize that it is unusual, and they have got to do unusual things to make it work. The relationship to the university—there are a number of those relationships, including teaching relationships, which I also believe are unprecedented in the National Park System, and they are very desirable.

We are going to be—if those provisions can continue, we are going to be providing for interconnections between the university experience in management and history and the operation of a museum which I think are very important precedents and very useful indeed.

With regard to the excursions, surely we need a mechanism that would provide to this committee or the Appropriations Committee with a regular reporting process under which the economic efficacy of extended excursions is something that is reported. Because it is unusual, and we do need to be sure that the desire, that the real possibility that those things can more than pay for themselves, that we certainly want to allow for an increased revenue stream to support this park.

We also want to be sure that somebody has carefully reported to you that those proposals have been analyzed, and I would assume that you would like a Park Service signoff on that, perhaps above the superintendent's level, to give you some extra additional assurance because it is so unusual.

Beyond that, Mr. Chairman, I would be delighted and Mr. Latschar—Dr. Latschar, who, in fact, has a doctorate, as I do not, in history—would be delighted to respond to questions both as to the management of this enterprise or any other questions that you may have. Thank you, sir.

Mr. VENTO. Well, thank you, Mr. Director. We appreciate your probing into this.

[Prepared statement of Mr. Kennedy follows:]

STATEMENT OF ROGER KENNEDY, DIRECTOR, NATIONAL PARK SERVICE, DEPARTMENT OF THE INTERIOR, BEFORE THE HOUSE SUBCOMMITTEE ON NATIONAL PARKS, FORESTS, AND PUBLIC LANDS, COMMITTEE ON NATURAL RESOURCES CONCERNING H.R. 3708, A BILL TO REFORM THE OPERATION, RESOURCES, AND DEVELOPMENT OF STEAMTOWN NATIONAL HISTORIC SITE IN PENNSYLVANIA.

May 12, 1994

Mr. Chairman, it is a pleasure to appear here today to present our views on H.R. 3708, a bill to reform the operation, maintenance, and development of Steamtown National Historic site, in Scranton, Pennsylvania.

We support the enactment of H.R. 3708 if amended with the changes included in this testimony.

Mr. Chairman, as you know, Steamtown came to be a unit of the National Park System in an unorthodox manner. We had not requested its inclusion and there certainly was apprehension on our part about this undertaking. On the other hand, there is an important story to tell at this site and, as things have evolved, it has become apparent that in Scranton there are excellent opportunities to demonstrate partnerships as a method to further the purposes of the National Park System. The relationship with the University of Scranton is an important part of this proposed partnership.

We agree that new authorizing legislation is necessary for this area, thereby repealing the language in the earlier appropriations statute. H.R. 3708 would formally establish Steamtown National Historic Site, in Scranton, Pennsylvania. The boundary would be delineated by reference to a map numbered STTO-80,000A and dated November 1991. The bill would repeal the Steamtown National Historic Site Act of 1986. It requires a new comprehensive General Management Plan to be prepared and limits the acquisition of lands within the park to donations or purchase with donated funds. It prohibits the acquisition of lands that are contaminated with hazardous substances and requires that the Federal Government be reimbursed for any funds already spent on hazardous substance mitigation within the boundaries of the site. The reasons for these provisions are manifest in the record.

The bill limits the number of locomotives that can be restored to operating condition to three steam and one diesel and restricts the Site's collection of locomotives and rolling stock to the current level. The bill prohibits the construction of new yard equipment or reconstruction of historic structures or objects. It prohibits spending Federal funds to provide access to any private for-profit structure. It authorizes train excursions to Moscow, Pennsylvania and prohibits the use of Federal funds for track, bridge, and tunnel maintenance or restoration. It limits other annual excursions to four and provides that they shall not be longer than 50 miles and requires that user fees recover 75 percent of the excursion costs. It authorizes the Secretary to assist in track and switch rehabilitation of Bridge "60" and Bridge "60 Wye" and authorizes cooperative agreements for law enforcement and rail traffic control.

The bill also authorizes an eleven member advisory committee, exempt from the provisions of section 14(b) of the Federal Advisory Committee Act, to provide professional expertise in railroad management and history and to provide advice to the Secretary in the development and operation of the site.

The bill prohibits the appropriation of any further funds for construction or development of the site without the specific authorization of Congress and freezes the operating budget at the fiscal year 1994 level. Finally the bill modifies the boundary of Delaware Water Gap National Recreation Area by substituting a revised map that deletes a railroad right-of-way that had been acquired.

Steamtown National Historic Site was originally established by the fiscal year 1987 appropriations Act, Public law 99-591, on October 30, 1986. Located in the center of Scranton, the site is adjacent to the central business district. We completed a comprehensive management plan for the historic site in 1988.

Currently there are 51 acres at the site in Federal ownership, all of which have been donated by the City of Scranton and private landowners. To date, Congress has appropriated $66 million for development of the Site, 99 percent of which has been obligated. Last year 156,000 park visitors came to the park from all 50 states and 54 foreign countries. Since it was opened in 1988, Steamtown has attracted 677,000 visitors.

It is with these facts in mind, Mr. Chairman, that we recommend passage of H.R. 3708. We do not recommend trying to undo what has been done. It is certainly appropriate and important that the park be formally authorized in a manner similar to the way other park areas have been established over the years. The park should be subject to the traditional budget priority setting process consistent with other units of the National Park System and upon the budget priorities of the Department of the Interior.

Section 102 directs the Secretary to administer the site in accordance with the laws applicable to the National Park System. We recommend that additional language be included that also directs management of the area in accordance with the Historic Sites Act of August 21, 1935.

We share the concerns evident in the bill regarding acquisition of property containing hazardous substances.

The bill requires the Secretary to receive reimbursement for funds already expended in cleanup before accepting title to any additional lands in the Site. We believe that the funds spent on cleanup may be eligible for reimbursement to the Federal Government under the provisions of the Comprehensive Environmental Response,

Compensation and Liability Act (CERCLA), which is the Statute that provides for recovery of cleanup costs from responsible parties. Final decisions concerning whether or not to file suit for reimbursement are made by the Department of Justice.

We agree that in the light of the record, a new, comprehensive General Management Plan may well be necessary. We recommend that paragraph (g) be amended to authorize the Secretary to enter into cooperative agreements with appropriate entities to further the purposes for which the site is established.

While we understand thoroughly the reasons for the proposal of section 106 of the bill, which freezes operating funds for the park at the fiscal 1994 level, we are concerned with legislative freezes on any park's operating funds. Furthermore, this provision would adversely affect the new facilities developed through the expenditure of $66 million appropriated by Congress.

The statutory limitation on the operating budget for this Site to FY 94 levels would not be compatible with the fiscal year 1995 budget request submitted to Congress. The 1995 request includes a proposed increase of $1.3 million in base operating funds for this site. This is required to allow us to protect the Federal investment that has been made and to open and operate the site as planned and developed, in partnership with a non Federal operating partner. We believe this is a better outcome than a legislative limit to the operating budget.

The long term operation of Steamtown provides us with the exciting opportunity to develop partnerships. We propose that a significant element of park operations can be achieved through an educational partnership with the University of Scranton, whereby the University provides educational and interpretive programs at the site. Visitors would be charged a reasonable fee for participation in these programs. This management partnership would allow us to operate the Site at considerable cost savings to the Federal budget and to forward our educational mission. This type of educational partnership being developed at Steamtown has the potential to become a pilot project that may have potential at other locations.

The bill establishes an advisory commission to advise the Secretary about the planing and operation of the park. On May 5th, the President submitted the Administration's first annual report on Federal Advisory Committees in accordance with Executive Order 12838 and indicated that the Administration will soon forward to the Congress a legislative proposal to terminate 30 advisory committees required by statute, but for which compelling needs no longer exist. Toward that end, the President requested the Congress to show restraint in the creation of new statutory committees. Consistent with this general policy, we recommend that the bill be amended to delete the commission.

Mr. Chairman, Steamtown National Historic Site was created and developed in unusual ways. When fully open next year, Steamtown can be an important element in providing American people with understanding of the dramatic and long reaching impacts of the age of steam railroading upon the economic, social, and political development our nation. We urge the committee to enact legislation that allows us to complete this understanding, to make it fully useful, and, especially, to open the way to partnership ventures that can, over time, reduce, not increase, its cost to the federal taxpayer.

I would be happy to answer your questions.

Mr. VENTO. Obviously, these hearings tend to rivet attention on issues that sometimes are out there floating around in terms of what is happening, and we were not aware of the proposal between, the University of Scranton where the university provides educational interpretive programs at the site. This is, obviously, within the authority of the Park Service to develop this type of relationship. In fact, I think, if anything, we encourage it. You agree with that obviously?

Mr. KENNEDY. Oh, yes, sir, we hope you do. This is what we are in business to do. We both are teachers.

Mr. VENTO. We take volunteers, and I think all of us think that the internship programs provide educational opportunities on site.

I think that, obviously, looking at some of the conclusions, I was a little bit surprised at some of the ideas. Is it a business school?

Mr. KENNEDY. Yes.

Mr. VENTO. That was the experience that we would be looking for.

So the point is, do you need legislative authority in terms of exercising this agreement or not?

Mr. KENNEDY. No, sir, I don't think so. It is possible that the very same cooperative agreement flexibility that is in the Historic Sites Act would be desirable just because it makes it a little clearer.

Mr. VENTO. You are talking about the fee issue. You are talking about the special permit fee. I think that you and I at least agree that we would probably do well to try and spell out in detail any fee legislation and/or some specific provision in here.

Mr. KENNEDY. Yes, indeed, sir.

Mr. VENTO. We have an unusual problem here. That is why I raised the issue with my colleague in terms of the operation and maintenance.

In terms of excursions, I think we should look to if they are going to be self-supporting excursions, no involvement of the Park Service other than the ownership of the engine. But, clearly, the expectation was that these excursions need some sort of a subsidy and that simply would balloon the operation and maintenance to whatever proposals would be initiated.

And there ought to be, and are, in the parameters of operating the normal park, some limitations in terms of what would be expended in terms of people that are coming to it.

Mr. KENNEDY. Sure. It would seem to me, Mr. Chairman, desirable along those lines that at least the Superintendent, perhaps the Director, should make a judgment in advance of such. You can get cash flow estimates of how something is going to work out. That is an expanded excursion that runs a greater distance. And somebody ought to sign off on that.

Mr. VENTO. What about giving this to a concessionaire to run and taking it outside the Park Service so we don't have the expense of operating these trains. They could do it since it is a money-making proposition for these particular types of ventures?

Mr. KENNEDY. That is exactly what we would like to do.

Mr. VENTO. You have the authority to do that now. I think that there would be nothing stopping you. I guess there is a question of using the rolling stock, the maintenance and some of the other things, but we have concessionaires using resources all the time.

Mr. KENNEDY. It is just that these hotels, so to speak, move.

Mr. VENTO. Well, they do. It is one of the points that is made here, is that they have repeatedly utilized the park, as the Park Service has now, under your direction, the operation and maintenance dollars to restore the engines. Are these a capital investment or are they an operation and maintenance type of expense?

Mr. KENNEDY. That is more complicated in this park than anywhere because it is true that part of the educational operation is running a living train. They are not just getting fixed and sitting there in mothballs. They are actually being used. And when you use something you have to fix it.

Mr. VENTO. Well, I would say that I understand that the fuel goes in them, maintaining hot engines, doing some of the other routine maintenance. But I think the thing is the restoration costs would seem to me to be a capital expenditure, but that has not been the policy and accounting procedure in the past. Why?

Mr. KENNEDY. I can't speak with any intelligence with regard to past practice. It does seem to me that there is a distinction in most operations between repair and rehabilitation for the purpose of creating an operation.

But if Dr. Latschar disagrees with me I would invite him to comment.

Mr. VENTO. Superintendent Latschar—Dr. Latschar, I guess you would prefer.

Mr. LATSCHAR. I wouldn't dream of disagreeing with the boss.

To date, the National Park Service's budgeting system has not given us any explicit directions, either pro or con, on the use of operating funds for the restoration of locomotives and cars.

As I pointed out in my response to this question to your staff, all parks systemwide are in this mix, whether they be built facilities. The question may be the definition of what is normal maintenance for a facility and what is capital maintenance, and that is a question that I couldn't begin to answer.

The bottom line is we made it clear to the Park Service as long ago as 1989 that because of the restrictions in the cost and the capital development program and because of the difficulty in using capital dollars, construction dollars, for restoration of locomotives and the extreme difficulty of doing that through contract, for example, we felt we were better off using operating funds for the gradual restoration of equipment which, No. 1, gives us the ability to hire and train journeyman locomotive and car mechanics which are extremely difficult to find on the street anymore but which we need long term to maintain the locomotives and rolling stock.

And, No. 2, of course, since from day one we have tried to make the restoration of the locomotives and rolling stock a key part of our interpretive program, so this is the one place in the Nation that I am aware of that visitors can come in and actually be escorted into our locomotive shop and watch these monsters as they are stripped down and restored and repaired.

Mr. KENNEDY. I do have one further comment, if I may, sir.

My own observation is what the Superintendent says is entirely right. The part of the education that is being done in this site is, in fact, real people working on real stock, and that is an important part of that process. Now, how you account for it we need to come back to you more systematically with.

Mr. VENTO. Well, I think the point is, of course, that it is an unusual number of dollars being expended for the restoration. Much of the early stage restoration is complete and a large amount of funding is still being requested for maintenance purposes.

But the concern is that there ought to be some articulation so that you know if you have got a general operating pot you can take dollars out of and use it for rehabilitation. That could be millions of dollars in a given year for that purpose.

And the fact is that the exploding operating budget is exactly what I am concerned about here, obviously, in terms of the future. That is why we are talking about excursions. That is why we are talking about limits, keeping hot engines. This is, Dr. Latschar, as you know, a very difficult issue.

And the fact is when you keep expanding it to use it for what is, essentially, a capital project and rehabilitation—I don't think there is any disagreement with the goal of having experience. But the fact is trying to marry those points together in terms of how you allocate dollars and how many engines should be restored, how much rolling stock should be restored, whether that comes in through voluntary contributions and so forth, gets all homogenized into an operating budget that is ballooning and will balloon in size. There is just no end to it.

We go to excursions. You go to rehabilitation of stock. I mean, these are major, major expenses.

What does it cost to rehabilitate a single engine? What has the cost been?

Mr. LATSCHAR. There is no specific cost factor that can be given for——

Mr. VENTO. What has the cost been for the engines you have restored? I am asking you a factual question.

Mr. LATSCHAR. I am sorry, sir. So far, we have spent over the last 5 years I believe $1.6 million. We have returned three steam locomotives to FRA-approved operating condition, one diesel locomotive, 12 passenger cars, and there are two more in the restoration shop this year.

Mr. VENTO. But do you have specific figures for the cost to the specific type of rolling stock in steam engines that you have restored?

Mr. LATSCHAR. I don't have those with me, but I could certainly make those available.

Mr. VENTO. I think it would be helpful to have that.

Also, I understand, a point in your favor here is that you have had volunteers work on those projects as well, is that correct?

Mr. LATSCHAR. That is correct, sir.

Mr. VENTO. The last time you came in we talked about most of the restoration, at least of the rolling stock, being done entirely by volunteers in terms of trying to initiate and reduce these costs. So I mean what is the full complement? What is the policy path here with regards to additional engines and/or rolling stock? What is the goal? What does the management plan call for? Do we have a GMP yet that is in effect?

86-965 - 95 - 3

Mr. KENNEDY. You do, but you have also required and we assent to there being a new one.

Mr. VENTO. What about the question? I am saying it is referenced in the general management plan, but what about the engines and the rolling stock projections in the future? You talked about what you have done. I am asking you what you intend to do.

Mr. LATSCHAR. We have got, Mr. Chairman, 35 locomotives in the collection, 88 passenger cars. Right now, my best estimate of the future plans is approximately two-thirds of that locomotive collection is going to be listed on the National Register of Historic Places. That study is under process now and should be wrapped this summer, which means that two-thirds of the locomotives would be considered national historic structures, which means that the Park Service would have its normal obligation to eventually maintain them and restore them to at least a museum display condition.

Mr. VENTO. You say 33 engines and 108 rolling stock?

Mr. LATSCHAR. Eighty-eight, sir.

Mr. VENTO. Eighty-eight, pardon me.

I think the point, again, Dr. Latschar and Director Kennedy, also my friend, Joe McDade, is you can see why we are talking about the dollars. And there is no way to predict, according to Dr. Latschar, what the cost is going to be here. We are folding it into operation and maintenance. Again, you can see my concern.

Of course, since they are on the register of historic places and since they are rolling hotels, in the words of the Director, it would seem that this is a rehabilitation. It should be a capital expenditure. The reason you have got some problems here, in all candor, is it is unusual, but it is also because of what has occurred here and what is likely to occur in the future. So we have got to get out there.

And, I understand there is a difference between whether or not they are going to be operational or whether they are just going to be restored to museum quality. There is a difference in terms of painting them up, oiling them, keeping them so they don't rust, and so forth.

So that is a big difference, I expect museum means less. Does it mean less cost than if they are rolling stock, Dr. Latschar?

Mr. LATSCHAR. Definitely.

Mr. VENTO. Mr. Dickey has been waiting patiently. Did you have any questions of the Director?

Mr. DICKEY. I have a question just generally, if I may.

Mr. VENTO. Yes.

Mr. DICKEY. Thank you for the time.

Mr. Director, I don't understand this idea about giving the assets over to a private enterprise.

Mr. KENNEDY. No, Mr. Dickey, I don't believe that has been in this discourse. We have been talking about asking for fees for entrance to a part of this or a large complex of stuff. And what was at issue there largely was whether we could cut down the cost of collecting that money and keep all of it to run the park with. It is not an unfamiliar situation.

Mr. DICKEY. I can understand how I missed that point.

Then answer me this: Is it possible for us to keep the park there for the people, for the entertainment of the people and for the general economy and actually have it run by businesses that bid for the——

Mr. KENNEDY. Yes, yes, sir. The colloquy with the Chairman about concessionaires on rolling operations, certainly that is the direction in which we would move for that. And in every instance where it seemed that we could cap the cost to the public by being sure that additional functions, however desirable, were treated as concession arrangements rather than Park Service-operated or federally-operated, we would do that.

That is sort of where we are. We are at the point where those additional—and there may be any number of splendid ideas that can come along from here. Many of them, if they would return some revenue that could also come back to the park, would be most efficaciously managed by a concession arrangement rather than by a Federal arrangement.

Mr. DICKEY. Right now it is Federal?

Mr. KENNEDY. Yes, right now, so far as I know. Is that right, Mr. Latschar?

Mr. LATSCHAR. Yes.

Mr. KENNEDY. So far, yes. There are some nonbusiness aspects to this, the educational parts, that are, of course, not Federal.

Mr. DICKEY. Why have we not explored concessionary alternatives before? This is my last question.

Mr. KENNEDY. I think mostly because it isn't up yet. The thing isn't finished yet. You haven't got an enterprise that is really fully under way that permits you to move much of it out. It is a fairly large—it is a large but fairly conventional Federal museum and park-like operation so far.

From here those questions become much more—will require some resourceful answers.

Mr. DICKEY. Thank you, sir.

Mr. VENTO. I think maybe I confused the issue because it is possible a concessionaire would use the locomotives and the rolling stock of the Park Service. In fact, today, don't you, in essence, have some sort of contract? You do not actually have Park Service personnel running those units?

Mr. LATSCHAR. Yes, sir, we do. Starting in 1993 when we returned on the track owned by the Lackawanna County Railroad Authority to Moscow, we have 100 percent Park Service staff and volunteers.

Mr. VENTO. There are volunteers?

Mr. LATSCHAR. Yes. It runs about half staff, half volunteers.

Mr. VENTO. Dr. Latschar, wouldn't it be possible to come to some contractual agreement, either in a concession or some other basis, to, in fact, pass this? Wouldn't it be desirable to do that in terms of what happens with these excursions in most instances?

Mr. LATSCHAR. It is definitely possible, Mr. Chairman. In my opinion, it is not desirable.

Mr. VENTO. It is not desirable. You would like to keep it inhouse?

Mr. LATSCHAR. Absolutely. We can run it with more flexibility and far cheaper than we can by contracting out to a railroad. In essence, we contracted with a railroad in 1989 through 1992 when we ran on the Delaware and Hudson/Canadian Pacific tracks. It took us to the cleaners.

Mr. VENTO. I think this is important. I am not someone who doesn't believe the Federal Government can't do anything right. I am just saying flexibility in terms of concessionaire.

Mr. DICKEY. Speak for yourself.

Mr. VENTO. I think there are some folks that don't have that.

Mr. LATSCHAR. If I could elucidate briefly, Mr. Chairman, when you are dealing with a railroad, only one railroad owns a track, which means if you are going for a concession contract, you are automatically in a sole source concession agreement, and the sky is the limit.

Mr. VENTO. I think that is right. If there isn't competition you have to make judgments. We talked briefly about that, Congressman McDade and I.

I wouldn't be opposed to but I wouldn't want to mandate that you had to. I think the concern is, Dr. Latschar, can we, if we are going to have excursions that go beyond the Moscow limit, which is of concern to Congressman McDade and others, can we, in fact, sustain a legislation or a language that would say there should be no Park Service subsidy at that particular point other than the use of the stock?

Mr. LATSCHAR. I believe that would be most reasonable and appropriate.

Mr. VENTO. You think that is workable and that such agreements could be attained and would be self-sufficient? That they would be workable? There is not much point in me doing it if they are going to come back and then be dipping into operating and maintenance funds for the excursion part other than for maintenance to the rolling stock. Once the rolling stock is maintained, if you have to roll 50 miles or 500, it is the same standard. Is that correct?

Mr. LATSCHAR. It is, basically, the same cost except for the cost of coal.

Mr. VENTO. In terms of making it, sustaining it for longer trips, I expect that those would be a special type of issue that would occur several times a year. It wouldn't be a regular thing. Or don't you know?

Mr. LATSCHAR. I would agree with that, sir, and I think the current bill which says four times a year is an appropriate target.

Mr. VENTO. So we have that in there already. Maybe we need to fine-tune that to make certain in terms of the amount of dollars.

What I am after is trying to limit the operation and maintenance, as you can tell. That is what is left. There is no use arguing; I could sit here and argue over historic fabric versus reconstruction. That is—we don't do Williamsburgs. I mean, they are nice to visit. I enjoy it. But we don't do Williamsburgs.

If we are going to start on that, then, obviously, we are going to have a lot more proposals in here and a lot more money to be spent by the Park Service if we are going to do them.

Some State park systems, my own included, have some wonderful re-creations of various historic sites. Out at Fort Vancouver, in fact, we have a re-creation out there, you know, which is very interesting. I had the opportunity to visit that. I was really hepped up about it in terms of some of the problems they were encountering until I encountered that it was a re-creation.

Mr. KENNEDY. And perhaps not on the original site, so doubly interesting.

Mr. VENTO. I think the thing that is even disturbing here, of course, is that some of the issues that were historic—I don't know if the site of the footprint is right with regards to Fort Vancouver. There is debate about that. But you agree that it is not. You are the expert on native American history, and if you really want to get into that——

Mr. KENNEDY. No, sir.

Mr. VENTO. Don't encourage me.

Mr. KENNEDY. No, sir. No, sir, I don't.

Mr. VENTO. One of the concerns here is that there is some historic fabric, as you have suggested. Some of the buildings are over 50 years old, and so they have been recognized, but there has been a disruption of some of the basic trackage that was there, there has been the footbridge which now is constructed with Park Service money.

But, nevertheless, it does superimpose something on the site that wasn't there before. These are actually inconsistent, again, with the Park Service use. You want to be user friendly and you want to get along with the town of Scranton, but the point is that we have an obligation, I think, in terms of what the Park Service response is to address that type of that problem. Is that the only way, Dr. Latschar, that access could be gained to the site? Or Director Kennedy? I assumed Dr. Latschar was there making decisions.

Mr. KENNEDY. He is looking at me, and I will look back at you and say, sir, that I think, however it got there, here we are.

Mr. VENTO. That is true.

Congressman McDade has been waiting patiently here without objection. You are free to ask questions or——

Mr. MCDADE. Well, Mr. Chairman, thank you.

I want to, of course, welcome my Superintendent, Dr. Latschar, who has been at site for about 6 years and has done a superb job. We are proud of him. We are proud of him as a Park Service dedicated civil servant who has done a magnificent job, and I am delighted to see him here testifying today, thank him for all the countless hours that he has put in our community on behalf not just of the community but of the Nation.

And I want to thank Director Kennedy for being here.

I did want to just ask one question. As a matter of public policy, Director, do you favor the statutory limit on the expenditures of operational funds?

Mr. KENNEDY. I do not, Mr. Chairman.

Mr. MCDADE. That is all I have. Thank you, Mr. Chairman.

Mr. VENTO. Under the Park Service criteria would Steamtown qualify for charging an entrance fee?

Mr. KENNEDY. Excuse me, I want to be sure that I understand both the question and response. I intended to respond to a cap in this bill. Is this what you were referring to?

Mr. MCDADE. Yes, that is correct.

Mr. KENNEDY. I have already stated in my written testimony that we did not feel that was the desirable way to handle this problem. I believe that that is better handled even in this circumstance in the appropriations process. That is the view we take.

Mr. VENTO. I understand that policy difference.

The concern, of course—and you know and I will be happy to yield to you. I don't want to cut you out in terms of the discussion here at all. The concern here is that the operating and maintenance budget has been used in ways that are unexpected and unprecedented. I think that someone could argue that it is an unusual draw in terms of how it has been used, as I had indicated in my comments just on the rolling stock and in terms of other issues.

It isn't just that. For instance, there was $1 million that was spent on the hazardous and other types of cleanups on the site. And, as far as I know—I don't know what the authority of the Park Service was in that instance. We can keep going through this particular discussion.

In essence, that is how it is. We have got a footbridge. We have the track ripped up. We have got other structures that have been modified by re-creation in terms of what was historic fabric which these are, in my view. And in my view they are departures from the normal National Park Service policy with regards to sites that they manage.

Mr. MCDADE. Would you yield, Mr. Chairman? I just wanted to say that the universal acclaim that has come to the Steamtown historic site has come to it from the people who have been there and have seen the Park Service interpret that era of American history. They are proud of it, they are interested in it, they are in complete support of it once they have an opportunity to see what the site is and how it educates people and what it teaches them about the history of this country.

That is to the great credit of the Park Service. I don't know that we need another comprehensive management plan, but I don't object to it. It just seems to me to be redundant because we already have one.

When we started this process, the Park Service held thousands of hours of hearings, inviting people from all over the Nation to participate in the development of the management plan. Everyone had an opportunity to openly comment on what is now an executed plan and the public is looking forward to the opening of the historic site in July 1995.

And the bottom line, Mr. Chairman, is that we must not forget that the public of the United States of America is being well served. Those people who come from the 50 States and the 54 nations that visit the site go away with unabashed enthusiasm for what they have seen.

I was relating to the Director that I had to do, as we often do, an appearance on C–SPAN the other night on the appropriations process. And as I walked out of the studio I met a young man who graduated from the University of Scranton, the very university we are talking about entering into a partnership with the NPS. And as I left the studio, the young man came up to me and he said, "Congressman, I just want to say thank you for Steamtown. It lets us focus on the history of our community and remember the greatness of the people who gave their blood to build this Nation in its industrial revolution."

That is the kind of impact that this site has on the people of America.

Mr. Chairman, the Park Service has done a superb job in meeting the public need and in trying to ensure that the public is well served, and I hope we don't lose sight of the fact that that is what we need to accomplish. Thank you, Mr. Chairman.

Mr. VENTO. I appreciate the gentleman's observations, and I am pleased that the public is enjoying this site, but I will maintain the fact that there has been a curious use of operation and maintenance funds to achieve the noble objectives that my colleague from Pennsylvania has articulated.

And the experience and the concern is, of course, as we look to the future—in other words, why are we doing or why are we asking for policy changes in operation and maintenance? We need to better define how these issues would be addressed in the future. I think that is important.

Clearly, the threat to deauthorize any type of a park unit is something that is unusual and unprecedented. But the issue here, of course, is trying to put this on a path where we can reasonably respond to the needs in the future, if it is the 88 cars, the 33 engines, if it is the excursion route, if it is further activity.

So I contend that dollars expended, re-creation of structures beyond just the maintenance and stabilization of the fabric, all of this in terms of visitors centers, certainly some of that would go on. I don't know of any other site where we have had the extraordinary amount of re-creation that has gone on. I would have to compare it to a site like Williamsburg in terms of—I mean, it isn't quite that much, but there is a lot of restoration and re-creation that has gone on here, and I think that it is a concern. And a lot of it has not just flowed in terms of construction type dollars but has been folded back into the operation and maintenance.

So what I think we need to do is establish whatever the parameters are. We can do it one or two ways. I could put an absolute cap on in terms of a proposal. That would do it. That is sort of a blunt way to do it, I think you agree.

The other is we can begin to sew together if we are going to have a user fee or a fee that stays in the park. We can begin to deal with the component issues that have cost the dollars, the reconstruction or the rehabilitation of the cars and the engines, and sort of put that on a separate type of a budget, and/or the excursion, so these are some of the elements.

On the usual issues I would agree with you, and I would agree with the Director. I think what he is speaking to is the normal type expenses in terms of operating the park; you shouldn't put caps on that because it is uncertain. They could go up or down. You could have more or less visitors. There are some unusual things that go on here.

But whenever we expend over a certain amount in terms of a capital project or rehabilitation, that automatically gets shifted to, in some instances, to the Denver service office or to another authority at the regional level.

What has happened here, Congressman McDade—and I think, Mr. Latschar, what you have done is you have avoided that type of accountability that would normally be pursued in the course of Park Service policy. That is my concern. That is where I am coming from.

In order to go forward and say we are authorizing $100 million here, $88 million of which has been expended so far, part of it operation and maintenance, then I have to offer something back as to what we are doing in terms of——

Mr. McDADE. Let me say, Mr. Chairman, that all of us appreciate your interest, and we look forward to working with you to complete what is a highly successful unit of the National Park System, and we look forward to working it out with you.

Mr. VENTO. I want to make it as successful as possible, just as the Director does now.

And I think part of that success of this unit would be its trying to gain and to limit and to address the operation and maintenance type of problem that has occurred here. But in order to do that, unfortunately, I have to parade out here all of our disagreements of the past. That is what you have sort of forced me to do.

I am trying to explain why we are doing what we are doing, and so, hopefully, we will be able to go forward.

I know you have to go, Congressman McDade, but I am going to continue with a few questions.

I had, of course, raised these issues, but I wanted to ask Mr. Latschar if he did or does have any concerns about the mall in Scranton.

Here we are with a park unit. There is a trans-boundary issue. You have Scranton. You had an historic designation or a mall there that would really modify it or an historic district. And here we are.

This is also related to the vernacular history of the working man, the blue collar worker and the types of merchants and others. Wouldn't it have been more desirable to have that maintained and some adaptive use of that particular type of structure under the Historic Preservation Act?

What happened to downtown Scranton when they gave the wrecking ball to this historic district? I mean, is this——

Mr. McDADE. Mr. Chairman, I can answer that pretty quickly. We got rid of a lot of vermin. That is about what was occupying those buildings. There was nothing in sight. The mayor worked his way through that for probably 6 years to try to breathe life back into a community that was dead. There was no opportunity, Bruce, no option to bring those buildings back. We had to demolish and reconstruct.

And, happily, we have one of the largest single investments that has been made in the United States of America there. The mayor can address it further.

Mr. VENTO. Wasn't there a UDAG project?

Mr. McDADE. It was a UDAG, sure.

Mr. VENTO. Mr. Latschar, were you present when that occurred? Did that occur when you were superintendent there? Did you offer any views with regard to the historic area district?

Mr. LATSCHAR. The decision, Mr. Chairman, that drew the boundary line and said, on the north side of this line shall be the mall, on the south side shall be the Steamtown National Historic Site, and the city of Scranton agreed to donate lands that they owned on both sides of that line to the respective projects was made 2 years before I came to town.

My marching instructions when I came to town, sir, at Steamtown was that the mall and its impact on the Lackawanna Historic District was a very, very sensitive and very political issue, both locally and regionally, and that the city of Scranton, the mall developers, the State historic preservation officer, the advisory council, and the historic preservation would mutually determine what would happen to the Lackawanna Historic District vis-a-vis the building of the mall, and the Park Service would have no comment on the local scene.

Mr. VENTO. Park Service would have no comment? In other words, you were told you couldn't make a comment on that?

Mr. LATSCHAR. That is correct, sir.

Mr. VENTO. The trans-boundary issue?

Mr. LATSCHAR. That is correct.

Mr. VENTO. Who told you that?

Mr. LATSCHAR. The current Director, current Director of the National Park Service, Mr. Mott.

Mr. KENNEDY. Then current.

Mr. VENTO. Well, one of my concerns has been the ability of Park Service personnel to address trans-boundary issues. Obviously, there are strong feelings about the viability of it.

The irony here, of course, in terms of Federal consistency, is that we have had Federal dollars being expended. I am certain that the issue was one that was agonizing both for the city and the community, based on the response of my colleague as well as the Park Service. So the mayor may have further comments on that particular issue.

Of course, the concern was that this went beyond simply the historic district. I don't know that the mall was responsible, but some of the historic track that was present there, that related to the Steamtown site but was not part of the boundary, was, in fact, also removed. Was it removed for the mall construction or for other purposes, Mr. Latschar?

Mr. LATSCHAR. Sir, the Park Service has removed no historic track.

Mr. VENTO. Park Service has not, but others have.

Mr. LATSCHAR. Let me be clear. The historic track that was removed was on the north side of the boundary line in the mall property itself. As part of the mall development, through a special use permit, the mall developer replaced two main railroad tracks for us, and, in essence, gave us two FRA-certified passenger tracks through the north side of our boundary at no cost to us. That was not considered a removal of historic tracks but just part of the routine maintenance.

Mr. VENTO. So there was some negotiating involved in that. Were you involved in negotiating that, Mr. Latschar?

Mr. LATSCHAR. Absolutely, sir.

Mr. VENTO. There was a trade-off, is that what you are implying?

Mr. LATSCHAR. Yes, sir.

Mr. VENTO. Well, we talked about the restrictions. Superintendent Latschar has been quoted in the paper as stating that unless Congress appropriates $2 million increase in operating funds for 1995, in essence a 70 percent increase, he will not be able to open the core complex next year. In fact, you stated, Mr. Latschar, that we may not be able to maintain the staff levels we have or operate the roundhouse or the excursions.

However, the administration is requesting a $1.34 million increase or about a 45 percent increase which I am sure will be very difficult to get under the circumstances, especially based on the 302(b) allocations that you are about to provide, is that right?

Mr. MCDADE. Well, we are about to do the 602's, and the Park Service budget for operations and maintenance will be $1 billion plus, and I think there is a place in there for this project.

Mr. VENTO. Yes. One of the concerns, of course, in that baseline is that the Park Service sent the budget up, I might add, including the entrance fee and fee type of increases in their baseline.

Mr. MCDADE. Would you yield, Bruce?

Mr. VENTO. Yes.

Mr. MCDADE. If you go through the budget there is $1 billion that the administration sent up for user fees, none of which may get enacted.

Mr. VENTO. We want to cooperate. I want to make it clear to you, as long as you are here on this particular subject, that we want to cooperate in terms of doing some things on user fees, not necessarily with a broad brush authority that each and every administration seeks with regards to these fees.

I am sure you feel that you know a little bit about what the impact is in terms of some of these fees and other costs that might be attributed. I mean, I am concerned, frankly, that putting in place and letting you have a fee at Scranton, as an example, would, in essence, deter the visitorship.

We have the investment. The last thing in the world we want to do now is put up some sort of limitation in terms of people visiting. If we are going to have it, they ought to be able to get in.

Mr. MCDADE. We don't think that would be a good idea.

Mr. VENTO. I know you don't. In any case, I think we run some risks. That is just an example, that they have entrance fees, user fees, special permit fees. Now under the 1935 Historic Sites Act, I think they have something else. But I think that we would be better off not to rely on that and keep this within the common strain.

But, in any case, the problem with the overall budget is that the Park Service went and cut this deal with OMB to retain some of the money.

Now, the other problem is, of course, they want all the money. They have already counted it all in the baseline. So I don't know how you can keep any in the parks. Before you get to first base, you have slipped on that. We will try to rectify that, Sid Yates, Joe and I and others, but I think that you are really making life more difficult in terms of that particular issue, and here we have some big increase.

Anyway, the differential here is significant. I mean, Joe thinks he can help. I am certain that he can. But the point is, we would like to have sustainable budgets, and you have obviously recommended that amount because that is what you think was needed, is that right, Director Kennedy?

Mr. KENNEDY. Yes, sir.

Mr. VENTO. Given the priorities, you think that is what is needed?

Mr. KENNEDY. That is what we could extricate ourselves for this purpose, yes, sir. That is as much as we thought we could get. And that is why we very much hope we can work out a fee arrangement that will make up the difference.

Mr. VENTO. We will work on that, whether or not we can get it up to $1 billion. I have never been more surprised by the amount of money people think they can raise through fees.

Mr. MCDADE. They said $1 billion Government wide, it is not directed to the park.

Mr. VENTO. I know, but the concern is we raise a small amount now from the fees we have in place, and they doubled the amount, and of course, without any process or realization in place, much less keeping it in the parks that collect it which, of course, exhibit A here.

Mr. MCDADE. I wouldn't want to prejudge the administration's likelihood of getting $1 billion.

Mr. VENTO. Not especially. It makes a difficult life for the appropriators even more difficult and for the authorizers.

Mr. MCDADE. If you will excuse me, I have to go over to the Appropriations Committee. I thank you for the opportunity to be here.

Mr. VENTO. I appreciate your presence and your work on this.

One of the issues here, of course, has been some of the trackage and repair work that has been done. To date, the National Park Service has spent over $3 million to repair bridges and tracks that they do not own, Mr. Latschar and Director Kennedy. We spent $3 million to repair bridges and tracks we don't own.

The right to use these facilities to operate an excursion line has been agreed to between the Park Service and the Lackawanna County Railroad Authority. It is my understanding that the owners of the bridges and tracks have agreed to maintain these facilities in the future. If this is the case, has the necessary maintenance to keep these lines up to standard been performed? Who is monitoring in terms of standards of these lines? Have they been maintained?

We don't have a maintenance and operation responsibility other than the initial expense we made, which was probably out of operation and maintenance funds—I don't know. Mr. Latschar, there were some specific appropriations for some of this. Do you know whether it was operation and maintenance money?

Mr. LATSCHAR. No, it was all construction money.

Mr. VENTO. OK, good. So that is not a problem then. So we won't be using operation and maintenance to maintain these, is that right?

Mr. LATSCHAR. No, sir, we will not.

Mr. VENTO. Are they being maintained?

Mr. LATSCHAR. To date they are, sir. As I said, we only started using those tracks in 1993, so we have got less than a full season of operation.

Mr. VENTO. Do you know what the likely maintenance requirements are or operation and regular maintenance on these tracks are?

Mr. LATSCHAR. The Lackawanna County Railroad Authority has budgeted $100,000 a year for track inspection and maintenance on this track.

Mr. VENTO. Just for that?

Mr. LATSCHAR. For the 13-mile stretch between the park and Moscow. That number may go up and down depending on track usage.

Mr. VENTO. Mr. Director, this is, again, the reason that we get concerned about what operation and maintenance can slip over into in terms of cost. Do they collect any fee on the consumer or the rider on that?

Mr. LATSCHAR. Their main revenue source, of course, is freight service that runs over those tracks.

Mr. VENTO. So that is used more extensively by others, but we have actually made a contribution.

What was the nature of that contract and agreement with the authority?

Mr. LATSCHAR. Which, sir?

Mr. VENTO. Is it in perpetuity, the use of these tracks?

Mr. LATSCHAR. Our memorandum of agreement, yes, it is down in perpetuity. In other words, it has no ending date.

Mr. VENTO. Do you have any charges that are due based on the utilization by the Park Service of such trackage other than the initial investment?

Mr. LATSCHAR. Yes. We have a cooperative agreement whereby we utilize those tracks for the excursion purpose, and we basically pay the Lackawanna County Railroad Authority the direct costs of two expenses that are caused by the excursion, the passenger excursion program. The one is the cost of passenger liability insurance which they normally don't carry since they are not in the passenger business, which is the brunt of the cost.

The second cost is the actual direct expense of conducting the extra track inspections that are required by FRA.

Mr. VENTO. What are the costs of both those items? Do you recall, Mr. Latschar?

Mr. LATSCHAR. For 1993, they were $53,500.

Mr. VENTO. For both?

Mr. LATSCHAR. Yes.

Mr. VENTO. This is a regular operations and maintenance expenditure, is that correct? Is this a regular operation and maintenance expenditure or do you pay it out of fees charged?

Mr. LATSCHAR. We pay that out of the interpretive fee revenues for the excursion train program.

Mr. VENTO. So you have a fee that you collect for the riders.

Mr. LATSCHAR. Yes.

Mr. VENTO. That does cover it? It is self-sustaining, is it?

Mr. LATSCHAR. It did in 1993 which, of course, was the first year we have been back on the shorter, cheaper excursion on the Lackawanna County tracks as compared to the longer, more expensive excursion on the Delaware and Hudson main line.

Mr. VENTO. Which did not, apparently?

Mr. LATSCHAR. Which did not.

Mr. VENTO. So the concern here exists. We still have a subsidy, apparently, is that right? We have a limitation of the bill. I assume that is because it limits the amount of Park Service money that could be expended on excursion routes, is that correct? How does that formula that we have in the bill affect your operation of that Moscow route?

Mr. LATSCHAR. If I recall right, the formula in the bill is that 75 percent of the cost of operating the excursion has to be recaptured through the interpretive fee program.

Mr. VENTO. You are satisfying that requirement?

Mr. LATSCHAR. I am very comfortable with that. Our target is to, of course, recapture 100 percent.

Mr. VENTO. Now the Park Service paid to fix the tracks in the past and did some work on the bridges and so forth. As I said, there was a considerable expenditure. Do we have any obligation in the future under this cooperative agreement to pay any further construction costs?

Mr. LATSCHAR. Not outside the park boundary, sir.

Mr. VENTO. So that was a one-time cost. So the regular agreement now in perpetuity is based simply on this track inspection and the liability insurance, that is limited?

Mr. LATSCHAR. Yes, sir.

Mr. VENTO. Well, very good.

That is the second bell. I think I have asked some questions. We will send some questions in writing to you, Mr. Director. And, Superintendent Latschar, we appreciate your response.

There, obviously, were some questions asked, some information requested, and we look forward to receiving that in a timely fashion so that we can move forward.

I will recess briefly to vote and then be returning. We will then hear from the next panel of witnesses, including the mayor of Scranton, who traveled all night.

We stand in recess.

[Recess.]

Mr. VENTO. Let's resume our sitting.

We have the panel of Mr. Thomas Schatz, the President of Citizens Against Government Waste; Dr. William Withuhn, the Curator of Transportation, National Museum of American History, Smithsonian Institution; and we have Mr. Ray Angeli, Secretary, Department of Community Affairs; and the mayor of Scranton with us.

PANEL CONSISTING OF THOMAS A. SCHATZ, PRESIDENT, CITIZENS AGAINST GOVERNMENT WASTE; WILLIAM L. WITHUHN, CURATOR OF TRANSPORTATION, NATIONAL MUSEUM OF AMERICAN HISTORY, SMITHSONIAN INSTITUTION; RAY ANGELI, SECRETARY, DEPARTMENT OF COMMUNITY AFFAIRS, COMMONWEALTH OF PENNSYLVANIA; AND, HON. JAMES P. CONNORS, MAYOR OF SCRANTON, PA

Mr. VENTO. We, obviously, wanted to get all points of view represented, but if there is some misunderstanding we want to make certain that we hear from the mayor. We can give you 5 minutes to make certain that you make your best case.

Mr. Schatz is the president, as I said, of Citizens Against Government Waste. We welcome you.

All your statements have been made a part of the record, so if you could give me about 5 minutes, then I will ask you whatever questions I have concerning these matters, and we will be on to other activities today. It is a busy day on the Floor.

Please proceed, Tom.

STATEMENT OF THOMAS A. SCHATZ

Mr. SCHATZ. Thank you very much, Mr. Chairman.

I very much appreciate the opportunity to testify once again on Steamtown, and I also very much appreciate your longstanding efforts to bring this project under control and keep the taxpayers from wasting even more of their money. We strongly support your legislation, H.R. 3708, to reform the administrative functions of the Steamtown National Historic Site.

As you know, Citizens Against Government Waste has been opposed to Federal funding of Steamtown since the mid-1980's. This historic project has received more than $80 million so far without being subject to the regular process of authorization, review, and competition with other components of the National Park System.

This is the most expensive train museum in the world for taxpayers, but Steamtown is not rich in value. John White, a former transportation curator from the Smithsonian Museum, dubbed Steamtown "A third-rate collection of trains in a place to which it has no relevance."

The critics of H.R. 3708 have stated that it is a poor attempt to micromanage Steamtown. But without some controls over expenditures, Steamtown will literally be a runaway train. By limiting Steamtown operating costs to $3 million per year, the National Park Service, which has a backlog of nearly $2 billion in operations and maintenance at other national parks, will be able to better meet its needs.

The original timetable called for Steamtown to open fully in the spring of 1991. Now the opening date is scheduled for the summer of 1995. This boondoggle, Mr. Chairman, just keeps chugging along.

While your bill limits the operating funds for Steamtown and makes other important changes, this subcommittee, as well as the entire Congress, should still take a good, hard look at Steamtown to determine the relevance, authenticity, priority, and real cost of this project before any more Federal dollars are burned up. I said this 3 years ago, and it is a shame that this same dialogue is occurring today.

The real issue today is the subject of operating cost caps. Mr. Chairman, your legislation does single out Steamtown on this issue, and you very eloquently stated why this is the case. Other national parks are not subject to a cap on operating costs, but Steamtown is not your typical national park or museum. It has not been subject to the authority of this subcommittee or the full committee, and that is bad public policy. That is why H.R. 3708 should be enacted. Your bill will at least bring some order to the chaos at Steamtown.

Again, Mr. Chairman, while the elimination of all funding for Steamtown is not part of your bill, we do continue to support cutting off Federal financing. Some people may argue we spent many millions, why should we shut it down now? The Congress did not buy this argument last year on the superconducting super collider. And if they can shut that down, surely they can get rid of the Federal funds for Steamtown.

Mr. Chairman, your legislation is the first step in putting a lid on this national pork scandal. It is perfectly reasonable to place this project under the auspices of the Secretary of the Interior and to seek donations and assistance from volunteers and other cost-sharing methods to restore locomotives and rolling stock.

I was certainly pleased to hear the Director of the National Park Service describe their interest in obtaining greater fees for the services of this park to help offset the cost to taxpayers. It is time for reform at Steamtown. For too long it has gone unchecked.

Mr. Chairman, I testified before your subcommittee just 2 days ago on the Presidio. While there are still many questions about how to move forward with the transition of the Presidio from an Army post to a national park, the parties to that arrangement have followed the process and are making a good-faith effort to limit the use of tax dollars.

It is distressing that we are even debating whether to limit funds for Steamtown while genuine national shrines like Yellowstone and Yosemite face budget cuts year in and year out. For example, salaries for some Yosemite employees have been so low that in 1988 they had to apply for food stamps.

It is time to halt this runaway train, and your bill, Mr. Chairman, will ensure that Steamtown no longer receives a free ride.

That concludes my testimony, and I will be glad to answer any questions you may have.

Mr. VENTO. Thanks for your testimony, Mr. Schatz.

[Prepared statement of Mr. Schatz follows:]

Testimony of
Thomas A. Schatz,
President of the Council for Citizens Against Government Waste
before the
House Natural Resources Subcommittee on
National Parks, Forests, and Public Lands
May 12, 1994

Mr. Chairman, thank you for the opportunity to testify once again on Steamtown. My name is Tom Schatz and I represent the 600,000 members of the Council for Citizens Against Government Waste (CCAGW). Since 1986, CCAGW has helped save American taxpayers more than $250 billion, with another $76 billion in savings over the next five years. With our national debt at $4.5 trillion, CCAGW will continue to find and eliminate government waste so more taxpayers are provided a better return on the their investment.

Mr. Chairman, CCAGW strongly supports your legislation, H.R. 3708, which would reform the administrative functions of the Steamtown National Historic Site. As you know, CCAGW has been opposed to federal funding of Steamtown since the mid-eighties. Since 1986, this historic site has received more than $80 million in development and operating funds -- without being subject to the regular process of authorization review and competition with other components of the national park system.

This is the most expensive train museum in the world, but Steamtown is not rich in value. John White, a former transportation curator from the Smithsonian Museum, dubbed Steamtown a "third-rate collection of trains in a place to which it has no relevance."

Critics of H.R. 3708 have stated that it is a poor attempt to micromanage Steamtown. But without some controls over these expenditures, Steamtown will literally be a runaway train. By limiting Steamtown operating costs to $3 million per year, the National Park Service, which has a backlog of nearly $2 billion in operations and maintenance at national parks, will be able to better meet its needs.

There are many reasons for the large expenditures to date at Steamtown. Above-ground hazardous and toxic materials were found at the Steamtown site. The Park Service spent nearly $1 million in 1991 to identify and remove toxic materials, as well as to conduct deep-core drillings in the railyard. The General Accounting Office has reported that other Steamtown site boundaries contain hazardous materials and that more comprehensive studies are needed to determine the full extent of toxic contamination and the cost of cleanup operations.

This sounds more like a historic nuclear test site than a harmless steam-operated train museum.

The original timetable called for the museum to open in the spring of 1991. Now the opening date is scheduled for the summer of 1995. This boondoggle just keeps chugging along.

While your bill limits the operating funds for Steamtown, this subcommittee, as well as the entire Congress, should still take a good, hard look at Steamtown to determine the relevance, authenticity, priority and real cost of this project before any more federal dollars are burned up. I said this three years ago and it's a shame that the same dialogue is occurring today.

From the beginning, the role of the Park Service has been ill-defined. The agency is not supposed to be in the business of administering a museum. Steamtown continues to be looked upon by curators as a congressional pork program instead of a transportation museum. When the city of Scranton tried to fund Steamtown on its own, the museum did not attract enough visitors to continue operations, so the city turned to the federal government for a handout. Taxpayers should not be financing a project which local taxpayers did not think worthy. Your bill would at least bring some order to the chaos at Steamtown.

In short, Steamtown has no national significance and should have never been administered by the Park Service. There was no comparative assessment of the so-called historic site, let alone an assessment of its "suitability" or "feasibility" for National Park designation.

The real issue today is the subject of operating cost caps. Mr. Chairman, your legislation does single out Steamtown on this issue. Other national parks are not subject to a cap on operating costs. But Steamtown is not your typical national park/museum. It has never been subject to the authority of the Natural Resources Committee, and that's bad public policy. This is why H.R. 3708 should be enacted.

While the elimination of all funding for Steamtown is not part of H.R. 3708, CCAGW continues to support cutting off all federal financing of this project. Steamtown is and will continue to be one of the most controversial National Park areas ever created. Some people argue that since we've already spent so many millions, how can we possibly shut it down now? That is a shallow argument. Just ask those members of Congress who tried to save the Superconducting Super Collider (SSC). The taxpayers know that their children are being handed trillions of dollars in debt because of pork programs like the SSC and Steamtown. If Congress can shut down the SSC, surely it can swat away additional appropriations for Steamtown.

The management goals and objectives for the site are to:

- provide a setting that recalls steam railroading while retaining the historic working character of the railyard;

86-965 - 95 - 4

- provide sufficient year-round facilities and programs so that visitors can understand the role of steam railroads in the growth of the nation while also providing hands-on, active experiences, including riding a steam train;

- preserve and/or restore steam locomotives and railroad cars at the site for exhibition, interpretation, and excursion; and

- use the site and rail-related artifacts to explain and emphasize the cultural/industrial heritage of the region.

But what are the realities? Retired Smithsonian Curator, John White, criticized Steamtown's significance by saying, "At best, this inconsequential collection largely duplicates what can be found elsewhere in better condition...On the basis of place in American history, no competent historian, in my opinion, would select Scranton and the Steamtown collection as, in effect, the national railroad museum."

Mr. Chairman, as I mentioned earlier, your legislation is the first step in putting a lid on this "national pork scandal." It is perfectly reasonable to place this project under the auspices of the Secretary of the Interior, and to seek "donations and assistance from volunteers and other cost-sharing methods to restore the locomotives and rolling stock."

It is time for reform at Steamtown. For too long it has gone unchecked. This is what a "huge sucking machine" sounds like -- a gigantic steam engine in Scranton. *Locomotive and Railway Preservation* stated in 1988 that "better train collections exist in St. Louis, Baltimore, Sacramento, and Strasburg, Pennsylvania."

Mr. Chairman, I testified before your subcommittee just two days ago on the transfer of the Presidio from the Department of Defense to the National Park Service. While there are some questions about how to move forward with this transfer, the parties to that arrangement have followed the process, appeared before your subcommittee, and are making a good faith effort to limit the use of tax dollars.

It is distressing that we are even debating whether to limit funds for Steamtown, while genuine national shrines like Yellowstone and Yosemite face budget cuts year in and year out. For example, in 1988, salaries for some Yosemite employees were so low that they were forced to apply for food stamps.

It is time to halt this runaway train. Other budget priorities should take precedence. H.R. 3708 addressees the abuses that are currently underway in Steamtown and will ensure that this facility does not receive a free ride.

That concludes my testimony. I'll be glad to answer any questions you may have.

Mr. VENTO. We have a statement from Representative Harris Fawell that will be put in the record, without objection, and one from Congressman Mike Andrews to be included in the record and a submission into the record of a letter from the Emeritus Curator of Transportation at the Smithsonian, John White, and that will be placed in the record.

[The information follows:]

HARRIS W. FAWELL
13TH DISTRICT, ILLINOIS
EDUCATION AND LABOR
SUBCOMMITTEES:
LABOR STANDARDS, OCCUPATIONAL HEALTH AND SAFETY
RANKING MINORITY MEMBER
LABOR-MANAGEMENT RELATIONS
SELECT EDUCATION AND CIVIL RIGHTS
SCIENCE, SPACE, AND TECHNOLOGY
SUBCOMMITTEE:
ENERGY
RANKING MINORITY MEMBER

Congress of the United States
House of Representatives
Washington, DC 20515-1313

WASHINGTON OFFICE:
2342 RAYBURN HOUSE OFFICE BUILDING
(202) 225-3515
CONGRESSIONAL DISTRICT OFFICE:
115 W. 55TH STREET
SUITE 100
CLARENDON HILLS, IL 60514
(708) 655-2052

**STATEMENT OF CONGRESSMAN HARRIS W. FAWELL (R-IL)
BEFORE THE
SUBCOMMITTEE ON NATIONAL PARKS, FORESTS, AND PUBLIC LANDS
ON H.R. 3708
STEAMTOWN NATIONAL HISTORIC SITE
MAY 12, 1994**

Mr. Chairman, thank you for the opportunity to testify regarding a costly misappropriation of tax dollars -- Steamtown U.S.A., located in Scranton, Pennsylvania. I come today as a Member of Congress, an advocate for the environment and the National Park System, a taxpayer, and the Co-Chairman of the Porkbusters Coalition, a bipartisan coalition of 74 Members of Congress, and 12 citizen groups, one of which is represented here today, the Citizens Against Government Waste. Testifying on the behalf taxpayers is never a popular job, and many-a-time, I and my fellow Porkbusters feel like the proverbial "skunk at the picnic."

Steamtown, U.S.A. was begun as a private venture in Vermont and was moved to Pennsylvania in the early 1980's. When private money ran out, further funding was obtained the old fashioned way -- the burden was shifted to Washington. Unfortunately, Steamtown bypassed the normal Congressional authorizing process and the usual review by the National Park Service, and was first funded in a Continuing Resolution late in the 99th Congress in 1986. To date, the project has received $69 million, though it has never been specifically authorized by this subcommittee. Each year since its inception, funding for the park has been non-competitively awarded, and earmarked in violation of an established Congressional procedure. This project is what my fellow Porkbusters and I refer to as "pork."

Mr. Chairman, you are to be commended for raising the issue of Steamtown's authorization before the Subcommittee, and I argue that this project should not be funded, particularly in light of our projected $223 billion federal deficit and $4.7 trillion national debt for Fiscal Year 1994.

The proposed budget for Steamtown FY1995 is $4.3 million. This is $1.357 million higher than this year -- a 45% increase. This percentage of increased spending is higher only in one other National Park, the Everglades, where federal dollars will save an endangered ecosystem. To contrast this with other national treasures, Steamtown receives almost 1/4 of the $17.3 million budget required to run Yosemite and 1/3 of the $12.6 million budget necessitated by the Grand Canyon. The money to fund Steamtown is being earmarked for a project that the Smithsonian Institution Transportation curator and senior historian called, "an inconsequential collection [which] largely duplicates what can be found elsewhere in better condition."

Mr. Chairman, I do not claim to be an expert on the National Park System, however others far more knowledgeable than I agree that Steamtown is not the kind of national resource that merits the allocation of limited federal dollars. In fact, historians and preservationists who assessed the Scranton collection discovered that a portion of the 37 locomotives and hundreds of rail cars and related equipment were not even American in origin-- 25% of the engine collection was Canadian and of that portion, only two pieces are considered "historically important" according to Michael Lennon, the president of the Association of Railway Museums.

The National Parks and Conservation Association, a group that functions as a watchdog over the National Park System views Steamtown as a "subversion of the public trust," which fails to meet the high standards of resource integrity expected of every national park area. These are not my words, but are the opinions and viewpoints of experts on the National Park System -- those who are dedicated to preserving our nation's heritage.

Mr. Chairman, we cannot afford the funding for this park. The yearly expenses for Steamtown are estimated by the General Accounting Office to reach $6 million per year upon the park's projected completion in 1995. Excluding construction expenditures, the park cost federal taxpayers $16.00 per visitor in FY 1993. By contrast, Philadelphia's Independence National Historic Place costs an average of $3 per visitor.

I commend the Chairman, and the Subcommittee on National Parks, Forests, and Public Lands for holding this hearing to discuss this matter. It is the job of every Member of Congress, of every American, to protect and preserve our country's heritage. For this reason, we must be ever careful in this time of national debt and limited budget resources, that every dollar spent, is a dollar well spent. Mr. Chairman, every dollar spent on Steamtown is a dollar that cannot go to other parks of national importance. For this reason, I support my fellow Porkbusters, the Citizens Against Government Waste, and others interested in ensuring that our tax dollars are being spent wisely, in opposition to further funding for this project.

Mr. Chairman, this concludes my statement, I thank you again for the opportunity to testify.

MICHAEL A. ANDREWS
25TH DISTRICT, TEXAS

COMMITTEE ON
WAYS AND MEANS

COMMITTEE ON THE
BUDGET

JOINT ECONOMIC COMMITTEE

Record

Congress of the United States
House of Representatives
Washington, DC 20515-4325

303 CANNON HOUSE OFFICE BUILDING
WASHINGTON, DC 20515-4325
(202) 225-7508

FEDERAL BUILDING
515 RUSK
HOUSTON, TX 77002
(713) 229-2244

1001 E. SOUTHMORE
SUITE 810
PASADENA, TX 77502
(713) 473-4334

STATEMENT OF CONGRESSMAN MICHAEL A. ANDREWS
BEFORE THE
SUBCOMMITTEE ON NATIONAL PARKS, FORESTS AND PUBLIC LANDS
MAY 12, 1994

Mr. Chairman, I would like to thank you for the opportunity to address the Subcommittee regarding Steamtown, USA in Scranton, Pennsylvania. As you well know, Mr. Chairman, I offered the amendment last year, during debate on the Interior Appropriations bill, which would have eliminated funding for Steamtown. I felt then that Steamtown was unworthy of receiving federal funding, especially considering the funding shortfalls that the gems of our National Park Service are currently experiencing. Both Yosemite and Yellowstone National Parks have had to cut back on public services due to decreases in funding. This, in my mind, is the tragedy of funding projects like Steamtown.

Mr. Chairman, I applaud you on your efforts to pass reauthorization and reform legislation regarding Steamtown. Your legislation contains appropriate provisions to curb spending at Steamtown and limit the Park Service's liability. It is a responsible bill which addresses many of the major concerns that I have about Steamtown.

Of course, I would rather see funding for this project simply eliminated from the budget, and I will be considering this when this year's Interior funding bill comes to the House floor.

Mr. Chairman, Congress has the important duty to preserve our history and protect and adequately maintain our national parks. And in these times of increasingly scarce federal resources, Congress must act responsibly.

That is why I offered my amendment last year to eliminate funding for Steamtown. This is not a unique historical landmark: our country already boasts of more than 200 railroad museums. Neither is it a pure display of our nation's rail history: more than 25 percent of the steam engines at Steamtown are Canadian in origin, not American. In fact, Steamtown has been described as a second-rate collection of trains on a third-rate site.

Interestingly, proponents have envisioned this project as a national rail museum, in the same vein as the National Air and Space Museum, which would bring back the glory days of our nation's steam railroads. Historians have noted, however, that Scranton is of only modest historical significance, asserting that Chicago, recognized as the greatest rail center in the nation since 1870, St. Louis, historically the second largest rail hub and already home to a magnificent rail collection, or nearby Baltimore, home of the Mount Clair shops, were much more important to the growth of the railroads and would be more appropriate sites for a national rail museum. With this in mind, I simply fail to see why the federal government should be funding such a project.

Actually, Mr. Chairman, Steamtown began as a private

venture. Only after Scranton lured the project from Vermont did private funding dry up and proponents turn to Congress for financial help. So, Congress carefully studied the proposal, received comments from the Park Service, and made a responsible addition to the National Park System, right? Wrong. Steamtown was first authorized in an appropriations bill in 1986, thus bypassing the normal authorizing process and the usual review by the National Park Service. The project has received nearly $70 million through fiscal year 1994, although it was originally authorized for only $20 million. This $70 million is enough to operate Grand Canyon for 6 years, and Steamtown's operation costs are ten times per visitor that of Grand Canyon's.

For fiscal year 1995, the Park Service has requested an appropriation of more than $4.3 million for Steamtown, a 39 percent increase from fiscal year 1994. Upon completion, the park will need in excess of $5 million per year for operations. This is simply too much to spend on a project that has been dubbed, "an abuse of the public trust" by the National Parks and Conservation Association.

Mr. Chairman, as you well know, I am as interested an active in historical preservation as anyone in the Congress. And, that is why I speak out on this issue. Funding for projects like Steamtown divert the National Park Service from its historic mission of preserving and maintaining great national parks like Yosemite and Yellowstone. Both of these parks have been forced to scale back services to the public in recent years. Such cutbacks include reduced patrols, longer response time to requests, and fewer interpretive services. The New York Times editorialized on this situation: "It's galling to let a boondoggle siphon even another penny from the Park Service's worthier, maintenance-starved projects." It is a travesty that we neglect these two true gems of our Park System so that we can fund Steamtown. Something here is wrong, and we must work to change that. Your legislation is a step in the right direction.

Thank you, Mr. Chairman.

5 May 1994

Mr. Bruce F. Vento
Committee on National Parks
and Public Lands
OHOB, Room 812
U.S. House of Representatives
Washington, DC 20515

Dear Mr. Vento:

I wonder how your committee can continue to fund the Steamtown National Site? This project has been discredited since its creations, yet the Congress has funneled nearly $70 million into a scheme that is nothing less than a national embarrassment.

I need hardly mention the criticism of this project in the national press. Articles condemming this waste of public money has appeared in the national media from the New York Times to Brian Kelly's book, Adventures in Porkland.

I could understand enlarging the Federal deficit for a truly worthy project but Steamtown is hardly worthy. Nor is it necessary. Existing tourist railroads demonstrate the fundamentals of steam locomotive operations and servicing-at no cost to the taxpayer. Far better railroad collections and sites exist elsewhere - facts I have explained before your committee and in the national press. None of these museums receive Federal funding and most subsist on very meager budgets.

I urge you and the other members of your committee to do the responsible thing - dump Steamtown now!

Sincerely,

John H. White

John H. White

Mr. VENTO. Let me then turn back to the other witnesses: Dr. William L. Withuhn, who is now the Curator of Transportation at the National Museum of American History at the Smithsonian. Mr. Withuhn.

STATEMENT OF WILLIAM L. WITHUHN

Mr. WITHUHN. Thank you, Mr. Chairman.

I am Bill Withuhn, current Transportation Curator at Smithsonian, and I need to point out that I am here on my own time, not speaking for the Smithsonian in any way.

I have submitted my prepared statement for the record plus an exchange of letters that occurred between myself and Senator Wofford last year, and I would just like to have those entered into the record.

Mr. VENTO. Yes, without objection, if you have those here. I haven't seen them, but they are relevant to the issue at hand, obviously.

Mr. WITHUHN. Yes, sir.

Mr. VENTO. Without objection, they will be added to the record. Are they attached to your testimony? Oh, they are. Thank you.

Mr. WITHUHN. Yes. In my 5 minutes of oral testimony I would just like to summarize.

The prepared statement also gives my qualifications, and I would refer you to the statement for those. I have a great deal of experience in management and, in particular, the management of for-profit railroad operations of modest scope and scale but very similar in scope to the operations of Steamtown and in and around Scranton, for that matter.

I would like to stress my observations about two things: One is costs, both capital costs and annual operating costs, and, second, the value to the public of Steamtown as an historical resource.

For 7 years we have been debating these issues, and I have been quoted in Newsweek and also in a popular book about legislative politics about Steamtown, and my comments have tended to center on the funding and the financial situation but also commenting from time to time about the historic quality of the collection, which I will comment on in a second.

My primary point of view, right now, is that that was then and this is now, and the question before us is what now for Steamtown, in light of the costs and in light of the value.

As to costs, given the scope of the project and given the scope as originally outlined back when the authorization occurred 8 years ago, to me the costs are quite reasonable. If, in fact, some good work had been done initially on the costs at the beginning relative to the scope proposed, I can't help but wonder how the debate about Steamtown might have been different.

But I also think that that was then and this is now. The investment has been made of over $60 million, which, as I say, I have looked at some of the costs and some of the line items involved in those capital expenditures and I, frankly, find them very reasonable in view of the work being accomplished, the kinds of buildings, the kinds of visitor facilities being built.

And certainly the issue of controlling the annual operating costs is very relevant, and as I think we have heard from prior testimony today that there are methods through cooperating agreements with the private sector by which those annual costs could be controlled and I think reasonably so and still maintain the high quality of operation.

So I want to focus, really, on the value to the public, from my point of view, as someone with 28 years of experience in operating smaller railroads and also 11 years experience as a historian with the Smithsonian.

I think the value to the public of Steamtown is enormous. It is not, to me, simply a train ride like other tourist railroads. I think other tourist railroads, in fact, simply operate with a kind of premise of a false nostalgia and such interpretation as they do is, to my mind, usually bogus. But, in fact, Steamtown is the only place in the United States and soon will be, even better, the only place where a valid interpretive experience in context can occur about the railroad industrial impact on this country.

This is a facility about working people. I think that is very important. It is about working people in one of our most important industries. Steamtown is one of the few places in the United States where the public will be able to learn by a direct experience something of the industrial life of working people who built this country.

Now there has been a lot of controversy about the integrity and significance of the collection. Given Steamtown's mission of being an active interpretive center where, in fact, some of the equipment needs to be used and, therefore, in a sense degraded because it will be used, that, in fact, the collection at Steamtown is entirely appropriate to its mission.

There are many other places in the United States and in the world where there are probably more significant museum-quality examples of historic railroad equipment, and I find that observation to be true but beside the point in terms of Steamtown. The objects, the specimens and their rarity or lack thereof is not the point. Steamtown is not a place of objects, like a museum. It is a place of experience.

And, as I say, I think the integrity and significance of the collection, in fact, is good. It is a collection that is from the heyday of the steam era in North America. It combines both American pieces and Canadian pieces, but the connection historically between Canada and the United States and the railroad industry has always been a very tight one.

So just in summary, I believe that Steamtown is indeed worth the cost. I believe that emphatically. And I think the annual operating costs can be effectively controlled in the way that the Park Service has proposed. I think this will be a very significant site for the interpretation of our industrial history for the American public and one of the few places, including other places such as Lowell, which has become one of the finer places in the Park Service for the industrial experience and its interpretation broadly defined.

That would conclude my oral remarks, and I would certainly be happy to answer any questions, Mr. Chairman.

Mr. VENTO. Yes, thank you, Mr. Withuhn.

[Prepared statement of Mr. Withuhn follows:]

STATEMENT OF WILLIAM L. WITHUHN
MAY 12, 1994
BEFORE THE SUBCOMMITTEE ON NATIONAL PARKS,
FORESTS AND PUBLIC LANDS,
HOUSE COMMITTEE ON NATURAL RESOURCES,
ON H.R. 3708

Mr. Chairman, thank you for the opportunity to appear at these hearings in regard to the future management of the Steamtown National Historic Site.

My name is William L. Withuhn, and for identification purposes, I am curator of transportation at the National Museum of American History, Smithsonian Institution. I appear here on my own time, not as a Smithsonian employee, and not in any way speaking for the Smithsonian.

To establish my perspective on the issues raised by H.R. 3708, I view the creation and operation of the Steamtown National Historic Site from two points of view: first as a historian of American transportation and secondly as a former small-business person and former manager of several profitable freight railroad companies. I am concerned with the meaningful and effective interpretion to wider audiences of the historical legacy of American working people, and I am concerned about the costs of such interpretation activities. Especially in activities related to railroad sites and the operation of those, I have had some 28 years experience, including a great deal of time spent in the maintenance and operation of a wide variety of historic steam locomotives.

I have visited the Steamtown site on many occasions, especially during the past year. I have gotten to know the professional staff there, and I have had a chance to see the plans for the ongoing site improvements and to become very familiar with the operations. As importantly, I have been able to talk informally but frequently with visitors. For the record, and for what is to follow, it is also worth stating that except for responding to a couple of questions from the dais during the 1991 hearing on Steamtown, I have never met or spoken with the Representative on whose list I appear today.

I was an early critic of Steamtown. In my judgment, much of its early planning was poorly done. With respect to the early years that followed historic site designation, that still is my view. I believe it would be helpful to be candid about that. When I was asked to evaluate the 1987 draft management plan for Steamtown, I found the costs -- both the proposed capital costs and the proposed annual operating costs -- to be vastly understated in my opinion. The rough cost estimates that I submitted back then, I must tell you, have been borne out.

It is now some seven years later. Is Steamtown worth it? Will the operation of the site be worth it in the future? From both perspectives of concern to me, historical interpretation and costs, the answer is emphatically, yes.

Steamtown is not a museum. It is a site created for the direct visitor experience of a part of our industrial heritage. As operated today, and as operated according to the plans developed for operations subsequent to the park's formal opening in 1995, the Steamtown complex will do what no other railroad historical site or museum now does: combine a valid interpretation of working life on a mainline railroad with direct visitor experience in full context.

The approach is fundamentally different than either a static museum or a tourist railroad. There are, indeed, a lot of tourist railroad rides around. Not a single one of these train rides has any concern with conveying a sense of railroading as part of our nation's history and social changes. The "interpretation," such as it is at such tourist railroads, is to my mind bogus. The only ingredients are a false nostalgia and an ahistorical, romantic view unrelated to the lives of real working people. So I do not see Steamtown as duplicating, in any valid sense, train rides already offered elsewhere.

The museum approach is also not Steamtown's approach. Ordinary museums, for the most part, focus on the objects themselves. Good museums go a step further and try to use objects to interpret something of their makers or users, but that is hard to do with static displays. Steamtown is actually part of an international movement toward "living history" sites, where the focus is squarely where I believe it should be, on the lives of people, not on objects. The U.S. is, frankly, behind in the development of industrial living-history sites and has very few of them, compared to other countries. It has been somehow unfashionable in the U.S. to celebrate working people and the industries in which they labored. Steamtown can help to redress the balance.

Steamtown's collection of locomotives and cars is appropriate to its mission. Certainly there are other museums with more historic specimens, but nowhere else in the country is the combination of resources -- specimens, site, repair shops, heavy tools, a large urban station under private auspices, and operational facilities -- as good for the interpretive mission of conveying what working life was like on the railroads, and for interpreting the connections between railroading and the rest of social and economic life.

There is also ample opportunity at Steamtown for cooperative agreements to both enhance interpretation and to share costs. An example is the recent educational partnership with the University of Scranton. And from the beginning, there have been cost-sharing agreements between Steamtown and the Lackawanna County Railroad Authority as to rail operations and track repair. In the future, I believe partnerships should be permitted to allow repair and operation of locomotives in the Steamtown collection that are of American origin. Steamtown has been criticized for the use of two Canadian locomotives, ignoring the fact that these two engines are noteworthy for their operational reliability and less costly to operate than the possible alternatives at present. But partnerships should be explicitly encouraged, at zero cost to the federal government, to sponsor the repair and periodic operation of some of the significant American pieces in the collection. For that reason, I would suggest amending the bar in H.R. 3708 limiting the number of locomotives that can be restored to operating condition. I also support the other amendments to H.R. 3708 suggested by the Park Service.

Returning to overall costs, both capital and operating, is Steamtown worth it? Recently, the Steamtown superintendent provided your subcommittee with a breakdown of costs and investments, from Steamtown's inception to date. Based on my experience with rail operations and with renovating or erecting industrial buildings, and based on my familiarity with the present site, the costs in that breakdown seem to me entirely reasonable. Given the scope of the project, there are simply no surprises here. Had some care been given to some of the initial estimates seven years ago, one might wonder how different the subsequent debate about Steamtown might have been.

Steamtown is today, and can be in the future, a unique and valuable national public resource. I believe in its mission. With the encouragement of cooperative agreements and other sorts of public-private partnerships, I believe that its benefit/cost for the American public will be great. Visitation will grow, and Steamtown will take its proper place as one of the premier interpretive centers of the National Park Service.

Thank you again, Mr. Chairman, for the opportunity to testify. I would be happy to respond to any questions.

Appended: Letters from/to Senator Harris Wofford, in regard to Steamtown, 3 August 1993.

HARRIS WOFFORD
PENNSYLVANIA

ENVIRONMENT AND PUBLIC WORKS
LABOR AND HUMAN RESOURCES
FOREIGN RELATIONS
SMALL BUSINESS

United States Senate

WASHINGTON, DC 20510-3803

August 3, 1993

Mr. William Withuhn
Curator of Transportation
National Museum of American History
Room 5010
Smithsonian Institute
Washington, D.C. 20560

Dear Mr. Withuhn,

In your capacity as Curator of Transportation at the National Museum of American History, I am writing to request your comments on the Steamtown Historic Site at Scranton, Pennsylvania.

The Steamtown Historic Site has been under development for several years and has enjoyed Federal-State-Local funding well as private support. When completed, Steamtown is designed to provide a working demonstration of our nation's railroad history and its role in the nation's industrial revolution. Although the project enjoys significant support, its historical significance has been questioned.

Considering your knowledge of the history of our nation's transportation industry and its contribution to the industrial revolution, I request that you provide Congress with your comments on the cultural and historical significance of Steamtown. In particular, I am interested in your analysis of Steamtown's collection of railroad hardware, the significance of Scranton to the railroad industry, and the historical interpretation of the Site.

Thank you for your assistance in this matter.

Sincerely,

Harris Wofford

NATIONAL MUSEUM OF AMERICAN HISTORY

SCIENCE, TECHNOLOGY, AND CULTURE

3 August 1993

The Honorable Harris Wofford
521 Dirksen Senate Office Building
United States Senate
Washington, DC 20510

Dear Senator Wofford:

Thank you for your inquiry of August 3, 1993, in regard to the Steamtown National Historic Site of the National Park Service.

I have followed closely the progress of this National Historic Site since its initial legislation, for it involves my particular field of historic preservation. My opinions on Steamtown come from two distinct perspectives. First, as an historian and museum professional, I look at the site for its value to the American public as an historical legacy and, more importantly, as a place for the effective interpretation of that legacy. Secondly, as a former railroad manager and small business person, I look at the site in terms of its management, its costs, and especially its value-for-dollar to the public. If I may, therefore, I would like to respond to your request, and especially to your third paragraph, from the above perspectives.

I was an early critic of Steamtown. In my judgment, much of its early planning was poorly done. With respect to the early years that followed NHS designation, that still is my view.

Much has changed, however. During the last two years, and especially since last spring, I have spent considerable time at the site. The Park Service and its on-site staff have worked hard to respond to the early criticisms that came from various quarters, and they have taken a planning and management path that I find to be first-rate. I have examined the plans and proposed exhibits for the new visitor center now under construction, and I have become familiar with the daily operations of the site. In addition, I have had many opportunities to talk informally with visitors.

To summarize my views today, I believe Steamtown is a significant national asset and that its significance will increase. Steamtown will become one of the premier sites in the nation for the public interpretation of America's important industrial heritage. It will engage the public as no museum of static displays ever can.

Smithsonian Institution · Washington, D.C. 20560

The site will be, and is already, a place of living history. Visitors can see actual railroad operations, with real people operating and interpreting the pieces on view. And that is the point. The approach is fundamentally different from either a static museum or a tourist railroad. The former is focused on historic objects for their own sake; the latter is focused on giving tourists a pleasant ride, with no concern for conveying a sense of railroading as part of our nation's industry and history. Steamtown is a facility unique in North America, focused on the relationship of Americans to their industrial past, focused on working people and their roles in that legacy, and bringing an interpretation of this fully to life. When it is finished, in my view, the Steamtown National Historic Site will be a major step forward in helping Americans from all over the country understand the industrial heritage on which this country is built.

There has been controversy about the historic character of the site and its collections, but I think most of this discussion misses the point. Scranton is one of the few medium-sized cities in this country where there is a combination of historic railroad resources located close to center-city, and where the historic physical connections of railroad to city still exist. Certainly there are other places with more historic specimens, but nowhere else in the country is the combination of resources -- specimens, historic site, repair shops, heavy tools, a large urban station, and operational facilities -- as good for the interpretive mission of conveying what working life was like on the railroads.

The unique quality of the collections is that, for the most part, they are operable. The collection consists primarily of typical equipment from the "standard era" of steam railroading -- locomotives, freight cars, and passenger cars. Their typicality is essential to the interpretive mission. In fact, it would be a serious mistake in my view to be operating unique, one-of-a-kind historical specimens -- those belong in museums in protected conditions. The Steamtown collection is one suited for operation -- and therefore, to me, of greater value to the goal of interpretation for the general public, as opposed to an audience of specialists.

As to costs, I believe that the public is being well served. Management of the planning process and of costs has been aggressive. Hard choices have been made as to what to preserve. The roundhouse/visitors center has been planned for maximum educational benefit, and from my museum management background, I believe the capital costs are reasonable. The operating costs, too, are reasonable and have been well thought out.

By and large, the US has been laggardly in preserving and interpreting its industrial history, compared to other countries. Great Britain, Germany, France, and even Switzerland, have outstanding industrial and railroad historic sites and living, operating museums. Internationally, the trend to living-history museums is well under way. Steamtown fits that trend. In this country, it has usually been unfashionable to celebrate working people and the industries in which they labored all their lives. Steamtown is helping redress the balance, in my view.

Visitors that I have talked to are enthusiastic in their reactions. They understand, I think, that Steamtown still looks rough around the edges. Amenities are few at this point, because the site is under construction. But already the interim operations are well received. And the high-quality interpretation, by experienced park rangers and guides, already adds greatly to the overall visitor experience. Visitation from around the country, I believe, will rapidly increase once the site is fully open and functioning.

"Functioning" is a fundamental part of the whole. The investment in the site can be rendered meaningless by unwise cuts in its operations. Care in budgeting is always essential. I believe the Park Service has exercised that care. I would urge those who are concerned to study the site and its operations, as I have, to better evaluate the cost/benefit in the interests of the public. A cut of operating funds at this juncture would be disastrous, in my view; Steamtown would then simply revert to being just another static industrial museum. The heart would then be cut out of its essential character and unique value to the American public.

Sincerely,

Wm. L. Withuhn

William L. Withuhn
Curator of Transportation

cc: Senator Arlen Specter

Mr. VENTO. Finally we want to hear from the other two witnesses before we get back with Mr. Withuhn. Mr. Ray Angeli, Mr. Angeli, please proceed with your statement. We have it in front of us.

STATEMENT OF RAY ANGELI

Mr. ANGELI. Thank you very much, Mr. Chairman.

On behalf of Governor Casey, I am pleased to offer comments regarding the significance of the National Historic Site of Steamtown. As the acting secretary of the Pennsylvania Department of Community Affairs, my department is largely responsible for the coordination of National Park Service initiatives with the Pennsylvania State Heritage Parks program.

Pennsylvania is keenly aware of its role in the preservation of America's industrial heritage. We feel strongly about the initiative that brings together the efforts of the many Federal, State, and local agencies working together in partnership to preserve one of the Nation's outstanding cultural treasures and historic assets.

Governor Casey established our heritage parks program in 1989. It was premised on the fact that Pennsylvania has nationally significant stories to tell about the role it has played in America's early rise to industrial strength and wealth through its diversity in historic sites, places, people, traditions, and events. Pennsylvania is in a unique position to tell the story to many people.

The Steamtown National Historic Site is one of those exceptional resources that has created a strong following not only from Pennsylvanians but also from visitors throughout the United States and foreign countries.

At Steamtown, for example, the special combination of historic resources allows visitors to relive the story of railroads and their impact on the industrial revolution in the United States. The 40-acre site was the home of the Delaware, Lackawanna and Western Railroad for 130 years, and no better site or collection of historic steam locomotives, steam era railroads, and equipment could better tell the story of the development and evolution of railroads during this past century.

Together with the nearby Scranton Iron Furnaces Historic Site, which underscores the importance of the early iron industry; the Anthracite Heritage Museum, which tells the story of anthracite mining; and the Lackawanna County coal mine tour, which takes visitors 300 feet beneath the surface into one of the original mines in the Lackawanna Valley, the Steamtown National Historic Site is the centerpiece of the effort to preserve and interpret this nationally significant era of American heritage and the natural and cultural resources of the first designated State heritage park, the Lackawanna Heritage Valley.

From the first time anthracite was burned commercially to melt iron in the hot air blast furnace, through the building of gravity rail lines, canals, coal breakers, trolley systems, and great factories on this site, a dramatic story unfolded. That story illustrates how the work accomplished in the Lackawanna Valley impacted on the institutional structure of our history, the American work force, and the urban development of the United States.

This effort inspired innovative delivery systems, new processing techniques, and a diverse industrial complex. Its successes gave birth to a very integrated coal transportation and manufacturing complex whose legacy is clearly visible in the region's landscape today.

Hundreds of industrial structures ranging from roundhouses to silk mills remain as vivid reminders of the valley's past. One only has to visit the region to understand the impact all of this has had on its people.

The immigrants who worked here established strong communities with solid values. They created neighborhoods filled with old world traditions in their homes, in their ethnic churches, and in their social halls.

To tell this story, a strong public-private partnership has been created. This is a partnership not only in shared responsibility but in commitment.

Our original heritage park's task force involved eight State agencies, the Pennsylvania Historic Museum Commission, the National Park Service, city, county, State, and local officials, and many other institutions, both educational and professional. Fueled by a grassroots effort, it was sparked by many initiatives like the National Historic Site of Steamtown, the Delaware and Lehigh Navigational Canal Heritage Corridor, and America's industrial heritage project in western Pennsylvania. Their ability to retell and interpret a significant era in American history is remarkable.

I am here today not only as a representative of Governor Casey but also as a resident of Lackawanna County. Like so many others who attended the public meetings to introduce the Steamtown concept, I realized the tremendous historic significance which occurred in Scranton and the Lackawanna Heritage Valley. It is the only effort where so many industrial themes come together almost within walking distance: transportation, manufacturing and mining. It is an opportunity to revisit history, beginning with the Steamtown National Historic Site.

The Commonwealth of Pennsylvania has invested more than $5.6 million for environmental cleanup, land acquisition, railroad stock, and track and bridge repairs on behalf of the National Historic Site. In addition, about $7.3 million has been spent or donated by local public and private entities.

The Commonwealth of Pennsylvania is grateful to the National Park Service for the contribution it has made in preserving this national treasure. The industrial heritage of both Pennsylvania and the Nation is being well served.

The Commonwealth of Pennsylvania strongly supports the continued development of the Steamtown National Historic Site in Scranton, PA. This effort will reinforce existing partnerships, help to save this cultural legacy and provide countless Americans with a quality educational experience.

Thank you very much, Mr. Chairman.

Mr. VENTO. Thank you for your testimony, Mr. Angeli.

Finally, we have invited the mayor, who apparently was not on the agenda, to offer a statement.

I note that I have your written statement before me. We would like you to summarize. It is a brief statement. You can read it if you want. Mayor Connors, welcome.

STATEMENT OF HON. JAMES P. CONNORS

Mr. CONNORS. Thank you, Mr. Chairman.

Mr. Chairman, I recognize your concerns and the concerns of the watchdog committees. As an elected official like yourself, we have only a certain amount of funds, we don't want to squander taxpayers' dollars. But I would like to speak to you also as a former history teacher, as a parent, and as a grandson of immigrants who came to this country and worked in the mines and worked on the railroads.

Mr. Chairman, we have an obligation as elected officials to present the history of our country to our people and to the rest of the world. And when we grow up in an area like Scranton and northeastern Pennsylvania where there is about a million people, we take for granted the trains. We hear the train whistles. We rode the trains to New York City with our parents. We watched the freight being hauled every day. We saw the men going to work and the women working alongside them. And we took it for granted, and we don't see it really as history until we step back and take a look at it.

And so while I know that you are struggling to keep people's taxes down and to keep the budget in line, just as I am as a mayor, I am asking you also—and I know how proud you are of what the Park Service does for people in presenting our history because I have heard you say that. I am just asking you to remember that this is a significant part of the history of the world and the history of our country. And it is really the people, the people from Ireland and Poland and Wales and Italy that left their countries because there was no work and came here and helped build this Nation.

And so I would just ask if you—I know that you are remembering that, and I know that is a great juggling act that you as an elected Representative have to do.

I just want to address a couple of concerns. First of all, user fees. Every municipality, both small and large, and every governmental entity is turning to user fees and turning to private industry to help out.

So, just to give you a mundane example, we have six swimming pools in Scranton that we are trying to keep open now. And one of the ways we are doing it is raising the user fees somewhat so that we can continue to provide that service to our people. Because we are not just in the business of making money or paying for services, we need to provide experiences for our people. So, just on a mundane level, we are turning to user fees, and we are turning to volunteers to help out. And that is, on a much grander scale here, what the Park Service is proposing.

It is such a joy to see the mechanics coming from Poland and to work with them on our trains because they have the great expertise, and then to interact with the Polish and Slovanic people of northeastern Pennsylvania whose grandparents and parents came from that country. And so there is a great interaction now with the countries where our people came from as they come over to visit Steamtown.

Just a note on our mall, Mr. Chairman. Our mall was built very sensitive to the fact that it was next to the national park, and it was built with an industrial and a railroad theme so that it would not detract from the park.

Mr. Chairman, I was the community development director in charge of public health and safety. And these buildings, believe me—and I am a person who is very much concerned with architecture—there was no saving these buildings. Our fire chief was not able to let his firefighters go into the buildings anymore. Not only was the mortar turned to dust and crumbling, but the bricks, the actual bricks were crumbling.

We did not take down any historic buildings, and when we built the project we were able to actually preserve the most historic and architecturally significant buildings in Scranton. So we want to reassure you that we complied with all of the Federal and the State and the local architectural preservation rules and regulations.

I would just like, if I might, to read very quickly the statement that I have.

Two and a half years ago I sat here and heard a vision of the Steamtown National Park which I am proud to say is becoming a reality. The Park Service has created a living park which is bringing joy, pleasure, and education to thousands of people from every State in the Nation as well as from 50 countries.

As a child, I grew up with the rail industry and rode the train to New York with my dad for baseball games. All my life I heard the whistles and watched the freight being hauled to all parts of the United States.

As a former history teacher I know the value of teaching our children the heritage of our people and of our Nation. The men and women of northeastern Pennsylvania left their countries of Ireland, Italy, Poland, Wales and many other countries to build a better life for their families. They built the railroads of this country and worked the coal mines and gave their blood, sweat, and tears so our Nation could become the greatest on Earth.

It is right that there is a national park based on the steam engine. It is such an important part of our history and the history of the world.

And it is right that the park is located in Scranton. Our trains still run. The first iron rails manufactured in the United States were at the Scranton Iron Works, which is preserved and restored and is located across the street from our park. There is no railroad without coal, and there is no coal without Scranton, PA.

It is right that we build a memorial to the immigrants who left their homes and gave their lives to build this Nation. It is right that their sons and daughters and grandchildren all over the United States know the value of their contribution.

Steamtown National Park is a great national asset. Comments from visitors are extraordinary. There are so many people in our country who have been touched by the railroads and who are overwhelmed by a ride on the trains, a visit to the museums, and a walk along the tracks.

The people of the city of Scranton have made a significant contribution to the Steamtown National Park. Our financial contribution is almost $4.5 million. We have made improvements to the Moscow station, purchased and donated rail lines, relocated businesses, and invested many dollars in infrastructure improvements and police and fire protection. This is our gift to the people of our Nation. But, more importantly, it is acknowledgment of the great sacrifice of the common men and women from all over the world who came here to work the mines, build the railroads, and make this country great.

Mr. Chairman, I am very grateful to you for giving us an opportunity to state our case. Thank you.

Mr. VENTO. It is important that you have that opportunity.

The purpose of the hearing obviously was the proposal before us, but what has come up now is the issue of a type of fee. Not an entrance fee—I guess it wouldn't be an entrance fee. That is for logistical purposes, and you don't have to know all of that. But is there anyone here that doesn't favor the fee or has any concerns about it or wants to make any comments about some sort of a fee arrangement for visitors to the site?

I mean, what the mayor is saying is that he generally is open to that idea. Mr. Angeli, I didn't know if you had mentioned anything about that or not.

Mr. ANGELI. No. As a matter of fact, we were in discussions with the University of Scranton and the National Park Service.

Mr. VENTO. So you had a discussion. What was your conclusion? Affirmative or negative?

Mr. ANGELI. I think we are in agreement with that. You mentioned something——

Mr. VENTO. It is probably unfair, but I think you had mentioned it in your testimony, Mr. Withuhn. You had mentioned the fee issue in your comments, too, and said——

Mr. WITHUHN. Well, not directly, sir. I mentioned cooperative agreements, something I have observed in the Park Service. But certainly as not a member of the Park Service, I am not an expert on that mechanism.

Mr. VENTO. You are declining to comment.

Mr. Schatz, you had mentioned it.

Mr. SCHATZ. Well, certainly, Mr. Chairman, anything, again, that would relieve the burden from taxpayers and, of course, placing fees or increasing fees at national park units has been one way to not only help the parks but help the bottom line of the deficit.

Mr. VENTO. We have generally tried to look at urban parks in a different capacity in the sense that we think there is a lot of utilization that goes on that might be impacted by virtue of a destination park like Yellowstone, Yosemite, maybe even something like Acadia. They are a destination parks where someone drives to them, and individuals are likely to face that fee. They face a lot of other expenditures in terms of hotel, housing, and so forth.

But urban parks represent a special challenge because, clearly, a lot of people go through an urban park. But the question is whether or not they would pay or be discouraged. What would be worse than having this park with all these dollars invested and then not using it? You know, sort of having some sort of limitation that would exclude people, that is the concern.

I mean, if you look at the excursion routes and the excursion activity simply because there is a cost associated with it, it has an impact. We are not talking about something incidental like we might have for 50 cents or something at the Smithsonian if you want to go to the Air and Space Museum and see the program. We are talking about something here that would be more substantial. That is the concern we have.

The Park Service keeps rolling out these numbers in terms of fees generally, and there is no projection as to what the market impact would be. And the concern is that that doesn't lead us to a real solution.

But if somebody gets a comfort level out of this and I can obtain what I want in terms of an operating certainty with regards to this, that is where we are going. Is there anyone here that disagrees with the need to have certainty with regards to the operations' budget of Steamtown in terms of keeping it within a certain framework?

Mr. ANGELI. I am not to comment on the dollars of the issue, but you mentioned something earlier in your discussion, two things really, when you talked about stewardship and partnership and you talked about the challenge of urban parks. You know, if we are going to develop sites like the national historic site in an urban area, the partnerships are what really needs to be created with historic preservation, with universities, with education, with private industry.

And I think the second part of that, the stewardship, it comes from the expertise of the National Park Service and our relationship with those people because they are the ones that can lay out the dollars that are required for us to be able to continue this. And it is our part to develop those partnerships that will support that.

Mr. VENTO. That is key because we want consistency from State to State. What is historic in Minnesota ought to be historic in Pennsylvania or California or Alaska. And that has been one of the great virtues—actually, we get quite a bargain on that because through the State historic preservation offices, we leverage a lot of activities and maintain that consistency. And so we are well aware of that role.

And, of course, the question here is when you have a lot of privately owned activity and some that might even result in economic development making money—that is not the case with the Steamtown site, but you have a lot of historic sites like that—it, obviously, means that it is privately owned.

We are not going to buy Wheeling, WV, as an example. I mean, they are not for sale, I guess, first of all. But Lowell is sort of, I think, an exception.

Some of you have raised the question of Lowell. Mr. Withuhn, you have raised that question. One other witness today raised that issue with regards to the issue of reconstruction. Do you believe that there has been an inordinate amount of reconstruction or a lot of reconstruction, re-creation of buildings at Lowell?

My impression was that the buildings were there and that they have been put to adaptive use, that there isn't a lot of reconstruction at Lowell, that the fabric was present, the historic fabric. You understand what I am talking about, do you not?

Mr. WITHUHN. Indeed, Mr. Chairman. I think, given what Lowell had to begin with in terms of the historic fabric that they had to use in that project, they did a magnificent job.

Mr. VENTO. No, my point is I agree with you on that, that was something we did with Paul Tsongas when he was on this committee and others have picked that up. But I mean the point is the amount of re-creation of structures that has occurred at Steamtown is unusual for the Park Service, is it not?

Mr. WITHUHN. Certainly the ratio of new construction to restoration of historic fabric.

Mr. VENTO. We have examples like Fort Vancouver which is completely reconstruction. It is re-creation of something that wasn't there. And I guess it is not even on the right footprint, according to what the——

Mr. WITHUHN. I would like to take the opportunity to point out that in observing the Park Service staff on site, while I have—the past several years, I have seen them do a magnificent and sensitive job with what they have to work with. I think the——

Mr. VENTO. The issue is whether the Park Service is going to take the units that we have designated, and it is going to do that degree of re-creation of structures. We would face literally tens of billions of dollars of investment that would be necessary. That is my point.

Mr. WITHUHN. I think that questions like that would simply have to be addressed on a case-by-case basis, taking into account the historical preservation issues.

Mr. VENTO. But the issue has been historically not to get into reconstruction of sites. For instance, if we are dealing with the native American housing or other types of structures at Chako and other places, it is not preferable to dig up some things. Because if you dig them up you are subjecting them to damage. In other words, it might be better to leave them in place for archeological, for preservation purposes. In other words, to take the basic fabric and stabilize it. That didn't happen at Steamtown, did it?

Mr. WITHUHN. It has. Indeed it has. I think that is where we are speaking in differences of definitions.

I would not classify the new visitors center and the serviceable roundhouse as historic reconstructions but rather new construction that preserves such historic fabric as is there very sensitively and then does this new construction very much in harmony with what had been there.

So the sense of the site is——

Mr. VENTO. We know we are going to get a visitors center, and that is going to be new construction. Every unit usually has a visitors center. They do some adaptive use of it when they can, but——

Mr. WITHUHN. In terms of the designs that I have seen for the park, the visitors center is incorporated in what is new construction around the turntable. So, in fact, it maximizes the ability of the public to see the railroad operations. There is historic fabric in the roundhouse, and every bit that has been original that is there. The Park Service people have done a great job in preserving that and pointing out that what is original and what is not.

Mr. VENTO. There is the recurring theme—and you know John White confuses me, I think, with the Appropriations Committee in the statement. I want to say that because, obviously, we don't continue to fund it. We haven't authorized the funding. We are trying to, obviously, limit the funding.

You agree, I take it, Mr. Withuhn, that we ought to address the operating cost of the park and try to address the ballooning growth, if I can use that phrase—or the potential misuse of it. Do you agree with that?

Mr. WITHUHN. I certainly agree that the issue of Steamtown's operations should be put on a stable footing.

Mr. VENTO. And to deal with the use that has occurred, as you have heard me describe it here in conversations, do you understand the problem that exists with regards to the use of that operating fund?

Mr. WITHUHN. Well, indeed I do. As a former railroad manager, I am very familiar with the problems in costing and, in fact, did the differences between capital investments and operating costs and sometimes where those overlap.

Mr. VENTO. Mr. Schatz, that is principally what I am trying to do. I can't go back and extract or rewrite history here. You understand what I am trying to do?

Mr. SCHATZ. Absolutely, Mr. Chairman. Of course, we are at this point. I know there will, I am sure, be attempts later on in the appropriations process to eliminate all funding for Steamtown. Again, given where we are, given the discussions, given I think the Park Service's inclination—although they, obviously, will not support it as public policy limitation—that we should look at how to be more predictable or at least have taxpayers have a better idea of what is going to happen in the future.

You mentioned the original cost was around $30 million. We are now up to almost $80 million. Given plans to maybe—I heard something this morning about having trains go to Canada. We don't know where it is going to stop unless your subcommittee and your committee which does provide limitations provides the parameters for these kinds of projects in conjunction with the Park Service, gets this under control, and we fully support that.

Mr. VENTO. We are trying. Obviously, it is hard for me to work with the principal sponsor and at the same time then have activities going on to do a slam dunk on the floor in terms of it, which may give you a day of good feeling, but the end result is that——

Mr. SCHATZ. Solution.

Mr. VENTO [continuing]. The appropriations keep rolling on with the limitations. So in the process of cooperating, you don't want to get co-opted.

I take it, on the operating expense issue, both Mr. Angeli and Mayor Connors had commented and recognized the goal that we have here and are amenable to it. Of course, your communities and the joint agreements that have taken place here will be key in terms of the University of Scranton. Is that correct?

You are nodding yes. Would you like to add anything to that other than an affirmative?

Mr. ANGELI. The only thing I would add I think some of the discussion I heard here earlier was moving to some cooperative effort on solving some of the concerns that they have on the site, and I think from what I heard earlier it seems to be a step in the right direction.

I do also want to say that we wouldn't be in favor of anything that would limit the ability of the historic site to reach its full potential.

Mr. VENTO. Well, I don't know. I think it is a question of defining what the full potential is at that particular point, but they have a general management plan, apparently, that is in the process of being revised again.

Dr. Latschar, did I misspeak?

Mr. LATSCHAR. We have no planning process under way right now, sir.

Mr. VENTO. It is stable now so we don't have a moving target? He has said there is no planning process. OK. We will look at that and see.

But the problem is, of course, that the excursions and some of the activities that are anticipated and joint agreement powers that exist can and do expand the function here.

One question I want to get to before I leave, and that is of you, Mr. Withuhn. And the issue is, of course, you said that you have run other railroad museums and you talked about this as being living history and interpretation.

But if you talk about the basic fabric, the collection of engines and so forth that is here, even though I note that you pay special attention to the professionalism of the Park Service of doing the interpretation—and I don't disagree with that. But that isn't the basis. That isn't one of the four factors in which we designate units of the National Park System.

Interpretation and the quality of interpretation, I guess, we take for granted if the Park Service is going to run it. In fact, it is one of the qualities and one of the characteristics that we want to try and keep in place, and I am pleased to hear the positive comments about the great job they are doing.

I, too, Mayor Connors, as a science teacher actually had to teach history on occasions. My task was a little more difficult than yours because I had to go to south Minneapolis, which was principally Scandinavian, and teach about Christopher Columbus discovering America. They had some notions about this fellow named Leif Eriksson, and they seemed to not be easily swayed by the history book or the other facts before us. And so the Norwegians and others remained adamant in their view.

And, in any case, one of the issues is, does the Steamtown, which is largely reconstruction, have this transcendent importance based on the types of qualities that really exist nationwide with regard to rails? What are we going to have to do? We have several units now in western Pennsylvania as an example that some—none, obviously, with the living history aspects, but that really is based upon having the resources.

I am certain that all of you would say any cultural or historic resource should be interpreted that way, but the extraordinary expense, of course, of doing that would preclude that type of park system type of operation.

There are a lot of private railroads that have been done. They may not be interpreted properly. I don't know. I mean, that is the point. There are resources at least as great or equal to what we are talking about here. Is that not correct, Mr. Withuhn?

Mr. WITHUHN. There are certainly more historic specimens, even in the State of Pennsylvania, in the history of railroad technology. But I just would point out that the collection at Steamtown is what it is. It includes a large number of American pieces that are certainly relevant to the northeast. Those pieces presently are not conserved and I don't think are contemplated for operation.

Mr. VENTO. Well, I think the context in which—you know, a text without context is pretext. So, obviously, we have to talk about what they are doing and the work of the Park Service.

We very quickly roll into the interpretation and the superior job and so forth that is done. I understand the rationale, but it does result in some circular discussion of the issue that is before us. And the question in terms of whether the basic fabric is there, and what is going to be done to remedy that. The resources have been invested.

We are where we are today, as has been repeated, but it is necessary for me to go through that to discover or to set a path as to what type of path we are going to be on tomorrow in terms of putting things back on track that provides some certainty and predictability as to where we are going to end up. If you don't know where you are going, I guess then any road will do, but I think that we ought to have and should have some greater certainty in this process. And during the authorization activity this year, hopefully, we can get that done and work cooperatively and achieve a solid public interest result.

I thank all of you for your contribution. I have to go vote, and I won't keep you any longer, but we may have some written questions that we will submit to you later as they occurred in committee.

We appreciate your cooperation and effort today. Thank you.

Mr. WITHUHN. Mr. Chairman, I would be happy to work with you on any historical issues and the historicity of the collection.

Mr. VENTO. The meeting stands adjourned. Thank you.

[Whereupon, at 12:28 p.m., the subcommittee was adjourned.]

○

APEX
TP
9780160467127
76901945 – 37